S.O.S.: Spirit Over Shadow

S.O.S.: **Spirit Over Shadow**

Deliverance from Tragedy to Triumph through the Holy Spirit

Jon Kocmond

RESOURCE *Publications* • Eugene, Oregon

S.O.S.: SPIRIT OVER SHADOW
Deliverance from Tragedy to Triumph through the Holy Spirit

Resource Publications
An Imprint of Wipf and Stock Publishers
199 W. 8th Ave., Suite 3
Eugene, OR 97401

www.wipfandstock.com

PAPERBACK ISBN: 978-1-6667-0168-5
HARDCOVER ISBN: 978-1-6667-0169-2
EBOOK ISBN: 978-1-6667-0170-8

06/29/21

For my son, Nathan, whom I loved immeasurably,
though imperfectly.

For Nathan's brother, Taber, and sister, Elle Louise.
May you be blessed with God's peace on this earth
as Nathan is in heaven.

For you, the willing reader.
It is your desire to understand and grow within
God's grace that gives Nathan's death purpose.

And for God's infinite love that makes this all possible.

Contents

Acknowledgements | ix
Introduction | xi

Part I—**Nathan**

Chapter 1: Tragedy | 3

Chapter 2: A Beautiful Mind | 6

Chapter 3: Inner Turmoil | 10

Chapter 4: Cancer of the Soul | 14

Chapter 5: Inadequate Care | 22

Chapter 6: Head Trauma | 30

Chapter 7: A Perfect Storm | 36

Chapter 8: Spiritual Verse | 42

Epilogue 1 | 56

Part II—**Me and You**

Chapter 9: Shock | 59

Chapter 10: The Holy Comforter | 63

Chapter 11: The Downward Turn | 67

Chapter 12: Prophetic Words | 72

Chapter 13: The Valley of the Shadow of Death | 79

Chapter 14: A New Hope | 87

Chapter 15: Binity Me | 92

Chapter 16: Binity You | 95

Epilogue 2 | 98

Part III—**The Holy Spirit**

Chapter 17: A Sacred Home | 101

Chapter 18: A Kingdom Life | 107

Chapter 19: Divine Revelations | 113

Chapter 20: Our Treasures on Earth | 122

Chapter 21: The Spirit of Truth | 127

Chapter 22: Infinite Love | 132

Epilogue 3 | 137

Resources | 139

Acknowledgements

Writing the first part of this book was a cathartic exercise for me. As painful as it was, putting forth my emotions on paper somehow helped release some of my grief. What resulted though, was a chaotic spewing of loss and pain. When I look back at those initial messy, musings, I'm even more thankful for those who first suffered through those renderings with me. They were Revered Chip Edens, Reverend Michael Potts, Leslie Escue and PerMar Olin. Reverend Lisa Saunders was the first to give me not just a sympathetic nod to my grief but also an honest account of the work that needed to be done if I wanted to better convey my thoughts. I'm incredibly indebted to her for that as well as the overwhelming support she fosters on behalf of our church.

The work needed was significant and not something I would have imagined I was capable of initially. As much as this final manuscript adequately captures my journey through Nathan's death, is attributable to the expert guidance of my editor, Scott Noble. His poignant remarks are what helped improve this book into something I hope will help others. Opening our eyes to the issues of mental illness and suicide is going to be a long struggle and will take all of us. This book is my humble offering in that regard.

The second half of this book was difficult to write for other reasons. I was spiritually shallow at the time of Nathan's death. All of my blessings from this time come from the Holy Spirit working in me. Most often my writing process went like this: read (the Bible and books on the Holy Spirit), pray to God for clarity and understanding, and arise the next day with a clear vision of what to write. I pray that has resulted in a work that motivates you to seek a closer relationship with God through his Spirit. This, I hope, is God's blessing for you.

God has not just revealed himself in me, but also in all those around me. I am incredible thankful for the love of God, manifest in so many family and friends. The outpouring of love my family received in this most difficult time is too overwhelming to mention specifically here. Please know that you are all a permanent part of my heart, and genuinely reflect God to me.

My wife, Sarah, and remaining children, Taber and Elle Louise, have suffered alongside me. More than anything, I pray this book helps their grieving process. As much as we will always live together under this cloud of loss on earth, may they learn with faith and certainty that we will also be united as one in Heaven. We miss Nathan terribly. The love reflected in that pain is also what draws me closer to them now.

Finally, all glory goes to God. God the Father, God the Son, and God the Holy Spirit. Selfless, loving communion with them is what eternally matters. This book only exists as a small reminder of that truth.

Introduction

J esus came down to earth to save us all. This was a radical idea
at the time he was born. Not that he was coming down to earth
or that he was going to save us: for the Old Testament is full of
symbolism and foreshadowing of Jesus' arrival. But that he was
here for us all, for every last person. God was extending his Old
Covenant beyond his chosen people and extending that grace and
love to all his children—Jews and Gentiles alike.

Even today, it would be God's preference to reach everyone in
this way and truly save us all. Of course, not everyone accepts this
gift. Many fall short of a belief in God our Father and Jesus Christ,
let alone acting in goodness and love as a reflection of such faith.

As I struggled mightily with my son, Nathan's, death, a
friend sent me a text which included a devotion by Pastor John
Piper. The "Piper," as you will learn, had become a powerful name
for God in my life, signaling that God was present. And so for me,
this message came straight from God.

The key verse in this devotion spoke directly to me. It was
Genesis 50:20: "As for you [Satan], you meant evil against me, but
God meant it for good in order to bring about this present result,
to preserve many people alive."

I first thought that only if Nathan's death could somehow
lead to the direct enlightenment and salvation of everyone would
it be worth my family's loss. Of course, this was not realistic or
possible. God would have sent his son if it was only to save one

person: you. Jesus would have sacrificed everything for just one of his lost sheep.

My goals today are much simpler. Maybe sharing Nathan's story will help break down the stigma of mental illness. Perhaps it will raise awareness to the tragedy of suicide and its increasing rates, especially among our youth. I certainly hope to shed light on Nathan's suffering and my ineffectiveness in recognizing and dealing with his depression preemptively.

As a pediatrician, I continue to struggle with how to help my patients. There are better ways to care for our children. And there are effective ways to treat depression and prevent suicide.

I will dare to branch into the spiritual realm, because the story of my own reconciliation with my son's loss begins there. In fact, this whole story begins and ends with love.

The disease of depression took from Nathan that love for life. And though my love for him has never wavered, it is imperfect. For me, only God's love, which has since been clearly shown to me through the Holy Spirit, has the power to redeem all the evil in this world.

For you, hopefully, I can at least help you express that love more effectively to your family. I know we were all created from that love, and we all have it within us; we just need to find ways to better share it with each other so that it might outshine the darkness that causes too many of us to suffer.

In the end, this book is about love. It is also about faith, and the love that stems from that faith. That faith brings me hope for the future. Maybe this book is my calling. Maybe it will help just one person deal with the realities of depression and suicide. Maybe it will turn many toward a faithful life.

While I am a pediatrician, I am not a therapist or a minister. In many ways, I don't feel qualified to write this book. But I do feel the Lord has blessed this work, and has spoken to me during this time in my life. I have had many moments of "clarity" after praying and meditating on many of the ideas presented here.

And while I hope I've correctly interpreted the inspiration I've received in the writing of this book, it may contain errors and will not resonate with everyone. Still, it is my humble prayer that these words will bring some peace, understanding, and infinite gratitude to some.

God has prepared a glorious future for all of us, protected from the evils of death and despair, in perfect loving harmony with him and each other, and in community with everyone and everything. That is my hope, and I have faith in its reality. Let me show you how I got here.

Part I—**Nathan**

— 1 —
Tragedy

My son, Nathan, died by suicide on October 9, 2017. I'm not supposed to use the word "committed" suicide, as this might stigmatize his act. Sometimes suicide is labeled as criminal or purposeful. And so let's get one thing right from the start.

Nothing about Nathan's death is right, or inevitable, or good.

Nathan was a beautiful boy whom I loved very much. But it is critical that, when reading his story, you separate his character from his death.

Nathan's death was a preventable tragedy. It was a failure on his part. And it was a failure on the part of his family, friends, medical experts, and community. We can all do a better job dealing with depression and preventing suicides.

We *must* do a better job . . .

Nathan was sixteen years old when he died. Nathan's downfall into depression, hopelessness, and death is still difficult for me to comprehend. Nathan had emotional ups and downs as he made his way through adolescence, but it seemed to me and everyone around us that he was just a normal, hormonal teenager.

In his junior year of high school, Nathan transferred to a private school and loved it. The compassion of his teachers mirrored his passion for learning, and he was welcomed immediately on the football team.

Then during a game on August 25 of that year, he suffered a concussion. Six weeks later, he seemed to have recovered and described himself as "95 percent better" to the concussion specialist.

His scores on his cognitive test were back to baseline, and he seemed fine. Although he could not play football again that season, he was allowed to return to the team and attend games on the sideline. He seemed happy with this. I was overjoyed!

As we left the doctor's office that day, I asked Nathan if he wanted to celebrate with the family that night. He resisted at first, but eventually agreed to go to Top Golf with his mother, me, and his sister (his older brother was now in college).

That night, Nathan took charge. He got us all passes and told us what to do. We ate dinner, and I can remember praying as a family, standing next to our tee box. In a circle, shoulder-to-shoulder, arm-in-arm, we thanked God for Nathan's recovery and all our blessings. By the end of the night, however, Nathan became moody and stormed back to the car, angry with his poor play.

That was Wednesday, October 4. On Friday, his dark mood lingered, and he decided not to attend his team's football game. He no longer felt part of the team.

On Saturday, October 7, he went out with his old friends and seemed to have fun. Video surveillance, however, would later show that earlier that afternoon he had stolen a rope from a local hardware store.

On Sunday, October 8, he watched football with me. Sometimes when we watched football together, Nathan was animated and excited. On this day, Nathan was tired and withdrawn. That was not unusual either. Later, he couldn't sleep and came downstairs after I had gone to bed. He and his mother, Sarah, watched a movie past midnight. He then retreated upstairs, mad that the movie didn't really have a point.

Monday, October 9, was Columbus Day. Nathan had the day off from school and had planned to visit his friends at lunch at their public school. However, he slept in and missed that opportunity.

At 3:00 p.m., just after Sarah left the house, Nathan wandered downstairs and told his sister he was going to Boy Scouts early. He just left our house. By 9:00 p.m., he was still not home. He was not answering his phone, and we became worried. We called the police.

An intense search for Nathan began that night. Friends, family, neighbors, and strangers all helped. Sarah and I went on local television and made public pleas for information as to his whereabouts. A reward was offered.

We worked with private investigators and their teams, who delved into his social media accounts and broadened the search beyond our city and state. The FBI was called in; fliers were printed and distributed; a GoFundMe site was created; and throughout all this we prayed. We prayed and pleaded; we wondered and waited; we did not eat or sleep.

Ultimately, none of it helped.

Nathan's body was found four days later, on Friday, October 13, deep in the woods by a mushroom collector. Nathan was hanging from a tree in an area about an hour from our house. From the condition of his body, it was clear he had hung himself on Monday.

He did not leave a note, he deleted all his social media accounts, and had given us no clue as to his intentions. He had simply changed his clothes, walked out the door, drove away, and killed himself.

Nathan was gone from our life forever. We were left alone and empty, confused and lost. How could our son have spiraled out of control to such a tragic end? And with us alongside him the whole time, unaware.

To us, he was still that beautiful boy who touched our hearts with every beat.

Question: What tragedies have affected you in life? What hardships? Make a list as detailed as possible. It might just include everyday hurdles to your mood or dramatic life-changing events.

Action: Pray for those in your life who are hurting, sick, or deceased.

2

A Beautiful Mind

Nathan was incredibly gifted. His intelligence and personality were great strengths, but almost certainly had something to do with his downfall. His intelligence was easy to see and measure. His IQ officially measured 140. He easily got straight A's.

Emotionally, he was even more brilliant. He was caring, thoughtful, and very aware of his own and other people's feelings. In elementary school, he was always named a "Terrific Kid." This award, in a class of about thirty kids, was given to one student each month. Presumably, the student who best exhibited that month's admirable character trait.

Nathan not only received this award every year, but he also always seemed to get it in the first or second month of the year. He stood out for all of his wonderful character traits. Oh, such joy and pride I had watching him grow up.

His smile and personality brought joy to any room. He idolized his brother, Taber, from the start, and he always looked up to him. In one video from those early days, Nathan and Taber are storming a castle that I'm defending, set to rescue the imaginary princess and money. As we get ready to film, Taber is excitedly relaying all the details of this adventure to the camera. When we stop to ask Nathan his opinion, all he can do is smile. He beams a giant smile into the camera, and his eyes sparkle. He just stands there in his knight's gear, as happy as any kid can be.

A similar picture exists when he visited his younger sister, Elle Louise, in the hospital after she was born. There is Elle Louise in his arms; Nathan is fascinated by how she sucks his finger, and looks up into the camera with the biggest smile you can imagine. In that photo, there are actual sparkles in his eyes. He was our happiest child. Always.

One year, the big Christmas present was the Nintendo Wii. It was as much fun for me as our two boys. Our favorite game was Zelda, and since they were four and six years old respectively, they mostly cheered me on and watched me play. It was an epic adventure, and we spent hours working our way through the game.

When it ended, highlights of your journey were played to beautiful music. We stared in silence and realized the adventure was suddenly over. Nathan, then just four years old, broke the silence and summed up our thoughts in a few words, "This is really sad." Tears came to my own eyes as I realized he was right. He always was.

Movies were another passion of his and as young as he was, he always figured out before me and Taber who was the bad guy, who was in love, and where the story was going. I loved watching his mind work.

When Nathan was twelve, we went on a skiing trip with family friends. One of the younger kids was just learning to ski, and it was not going well. As we rode by on the chairlift, we could see him frozen with fear and tears in the middle of the slope. His mother was trying to help him, but was quickly becoming fed up and frustrated. We all assumed they were done, and we'd see them for hot chocolate at lunchtime. So we just skied on.

The next time up the chairlift, Nathan was not with us. On the way up, we looked down and found him. There he was relieving the mother and teaching the boy to ski. By the end of the day, the boy was skiing well, and they both joined us for the rest of the trip and had the time of their lives. Even at such a young age, Nathan was a hero.

Midway through his freshman year of high school, Nathan revealed to us that he was not working out with the football team in the offseason. In fact, he wanted to quit the team. He told us that as the season ended, parties had begun. He did not feel comfortable with the increasing pressure from his teammates to drink alcohol. We supported his mature decision to leave that environment, but it was not that easy for him.

Later that year, Nathan and I spoke of the pain he felt in leaving his old friends. He detailed to me how he had to find other friends at lunch, how he had to work to find a new place for himself. He was happy with his decision, but there was a good bit of sadness as he described the loss of many of his childhood friends. He was rewarded with a wonderful collection of new friends, however, and he often enjoyed their company even outside of school.

The following New Year's Eve, those old friends were in our neighborhood. With one classmate's family out of town, they threw a big party in her house and trashed the place. Word got out and soon police helicopters were circling our neighborhood and searching for Nathan's scattered "friends." Nathan followed on social media as many of them were hiding out in various spots throughout our neighborhood. Many were caught, and the ramifications were serious.

We made our way to the house where police had many of the kids in custody. One by one, their parents drove up, got the full story from the police, and drove home. My friends and I lavished praise on Nathan that night for his character and forethought in making smart decisions. I'm not sure today, though, if he understood how proud I was of him, or if he just felt alone. That was January.

Sarah and I often referred to Nathan as our Boy Scout. He was every bit one. Compassionate, caring, helpful, kind, and brave. He gave his Christmas money away to charities and volunteered his time helping others. In his Boy Scout troop, he aced his technical skills tests and at a young age advanced to "Senior Patrol Leader," the highest officer of the troop. There was no doubt he could achieve anything he set his mind to accomplish.

Sadly, though, somehow his beautiful mind ended up being more of a curse than a blessing.

Question: What is it that makes each member of your family special to you?

Action: Tell one of these people of your good thoughts about them. Write an email or letter. Call them. Or visit them. Consider bringing them a present that reflects your appreciation for them.

3

Inner Turmoil

The way I see it now, Nathan's first problem was his brilliance. I have no shame in telling my other two children that Nathan was the smartest. Sarah and I met at Brown University, an Ivy League institution. Nathan was smarter than us too.

I can now only imagine the problems he could have solved as an adult. He certainly could have done anything he set his mind to; knowing his character, he would have done many, very good things for others. His intelligence was a great strength, but certainly had something to do with why he got depressed and how he handled it.

In fact, it has been documented by recent research that there is a link between intelligence and suicide. Martin Voracek has done a lot of work in this regard, and in 2009 published a study showing a direct link between a nation's measured intelligence and its suicide rates. Incidentally, those countries with higher suicide rates also had many other positive qualities, including affluence, lower rates of infant mortality and HIV/AIDS infections, and less violent crime.

The Office for National Statistics in England published a 2017 study that showed a higher rate of suicide in those with creative, art-related jobs. Tortured geniuses of history who committed suicide include Vincent van Gogh, Ernest Hemingway, Virginia Woolf, Kurt Cobain, and Robin Williams. (It should be noted, though, that in the English study, those with low-skilled, low-paying jobs actually had the highest increased risk of suicide).

Perhaps it is those who operate on the fringes of society (good or bad) who are at most risk.

I am still proud to say that in every positive sense, Nathan was an exceptional outlier.

Nathan was also passionate and compassionate. He was emotionally sensitive to all the problems around him. In today's world, as well as in his isolated teenage mind, that was no small thing. He treasured his relationships, and when those became stressed by his depression—when he no longer found enjoyment in others—it devastated him.

He valued the quality of his education as well. But that was another problem. Nathan ran away eight months prior to his death, mostly because he was not happy in school. Not because of his grades; they were fine. He was most frustrated and disappointed in that "no one cared about them, the students."

His teachers had become antagonists, working against students' good intentions. He found no relief or love of learning in his school. Taber, a senior at the time, was not surprised. "Of course," Taber told us. "In my four years of high school, I can think of maybe two teachers who actually cared about us. But so what? They don't care about us, and so none of the students care about their school work."

I suppose we shouldn't have been surprised to hear this. Taber was about to graduate, and his grades had been a reflection of his lack of concern. He was able to brush off that apathy and casually coexist with it. Nathan was not so lucky. He took this all personally.

We knew there was a problem with the attitude in the school system, and it started at the top. When Nathan was in eighth grade, he was the captain of the rugby team. Their season was in the winter, but they all wanted to continue playing in the spring as well, as that option existed in their league.

Nathan and the other captain approached the principal with this idea, and the first response they got was that there was not enough field space for this. One look behind the school where multiple fields existed convinced them this was not really a problem.

So Nathan and the other captain wrote a petition to continue the rugby season. They got more than one hundred students to sign it, and presented their proposal to the principal once again. This time her response was to rip up the petition, throw it in the trash in front of them, and flatly state that the extended season was not going to happen. For a principal who guides young minds, who glorified in the school's anti-bullying policies, and who set the example for the other teachers, this was appalling to us.

In high school, it seemed even worse. Every week our boys related one similar story after another. The teachers delivered tests on subject matter they did not teach, they did not show up for extra help, and graded papers with appalling inconsistencies. It really should not have been much of a shock that Nathan was losing his patience with this system. He understood all too well his place there and was not happy about it.

I'm not sure if this is where Nathan's thoughts of helplessness and worthlessness started, but I'm sure it did not help. We sympathized with him as this all came to a head. We actually offered to take him out of school if he wished. We knew he would thrive in whatever environment we placed him. Sarah and I went so far as to offer to fund Nathan's "running away" if that was what he desired. We were willing to do anything to make him happy.

In the end, he decided to finish out his sophomore year and transfer to another school the following year. We encouraged him to let those frustrations roll off him, and it seemed to work. He finished the year easily, and seemed to be turning the corner.

Maybe Nathan expected everything to work out just as he would have done it. In that sense, nothing seemed to measure up. I think also the fact that he couldn't identify his passion in life—a concept that was emphasized as he prepared for college and life beyond, further saddened him. I think he felt that if he couldn't find joy in his school, home, activities, friends, and family, then he was just not worth much as a person. He not only understood the injustices around him but was also disturbed by them.

As a teenager, Nathan did not express his depression well enough to others. And as things worsened, he shut down even more. This only exacerbated his problems. I would guess he was embarrassed, ashamed, and guilty for not being able to handle this himself. I suppose, like most teenagers, he initially thought he was invulnerable. He tried to fix it himself, thought too much about it all, and got worse. He did not see openness, vulnerability, and the courage to open up about things as traits of a strong character. And so he suffered alone.

I'm sure he was as confused about all this as we are now. It certainly didn't help that his psychologists did not recognize this as a problem, a disease that needed addressing and could be helped. Rather, the message I think he got from those "experts" was that this was just his mind, and he was stuck with it forever. How wrong they were.

Depression must be a downward spiral. His feelings of worthlessness, remorse, loneliness, and hopeless just exacerbated themselves. And as powerful as his mind was, it was not strong enough to overcome the physical effects of these stressors and this depressive disease on his brain.

Question: What makes you uneasy about our society? What can you do about it?

Action: Watch a movie that takes you out of your comfort zone and causes you to see things from another perspective. My favorites: *The Pursuit of Happiness, The Fisher King, One Flew Over the Cuckoo's Nest, Rain Man, A Beautiful Mind, The Shape of Water, The Theory of Everything, Wonder, Remember the Titans, The Hate U Give, Get Out, Do the Right Thing, The Defiant Ones, Green Book, Pleasantville, Driving Miss Daisy, The Shawshank Redemption, The Help,* and *Hidden Figures.*

4

Cancer of the Soul

Nathan died in October, but our first sign he was restless was in February. On my birthday, February 3, he gave me a wonderful card that read, "I hope you have an awesome year and continue to take us on all sorts of different adventures."

Indeed, in the three years prior, he and I had learned to whitewater kayak, rode dirt bikes together, surfed, and went scuba diving in the Caribbean. Life was as good as it could be for an upper class, white American family. But then, one week after he wrote hopefully in my birthday card—one month after that New Year's in which we were so proud—he ran away.

He was only gone for three hours. He left the house at 5:00 p.m. for a Boy Scouts meeting, and at 8:00 p.m. his alarm went off in his room. Sarah went in there to turn the alarm off, and all I heard was her horrendous scream reverberating throughout the house.

Something was obviously wrong. Nathan had carefully organized his room, and to us it looked like it was made up for a funeral. It was neatly cleaned. The bed was made, and all his childhood scrapbooks were laid out on it.

On top of all his childhood memories was a note addressed to "My Family." Sarah could not read it for fear of what the note said. We thought he was gone, and the note did not offer us much hope.

It read in part, "I have decided to leave home and see what the world has to offer me. I've been thinking about this for a long time and my mind is made up . . . . I am simply not happy in life . . . . This is in no way your fault. The last thing I want to do is hurt you. I have made my decision, and I am Never coming back. Please [underlined three times] do not try to look for me. I will only resent you for it. Remember me how I was. I believe I am finally Happy and Free. Love, Nathan Ward Kocmond."

I called him immediately on his cell phone. He answered and was home in fifteen minutes. Taber was as affected as anyone, and as I brought Nathan in the door, they hugged for what seemed like forever. We stayed up most of the night as a family, consoling one another. As traumatic as it was, it seemed like we would all get through this together. No one went to school the next day.

I texted a psychologist friend of mine that morning: "We almost lost Nathan literally and figuratively last night. We need help." Nathan was seen by him that week, and for about three visits thereafter.

I remember that first visit with the psychologist. "This is not a suicide note," he had said. And over the next month, the psychologist proceeded to convince us that Nathan was a normal, temperamental, and impulsive fifteen-year-old boy.

At the last visit, he met with Sarah and me and again reinforced that Nathan was fine. He was an "existential thinker," he told us; his thoughts were strong and deep but normal. I remember my response like it was yesterday: "If he's an existential thinker, then he's a pathological existential thinker."

I was using medical language to express that I thought Nathan's thoughts had crossed into the realm of being a problem, a disease. It was that these thoughts had so dramatically broken into his normal life that convinced me. The psychologist laughed at me, like what I was saying was cute and the furthest thing from the truth.

Looking back, I think Nathan's downward spiral began with this episode, as did our all-too-relaxed attitude toward his struggles. I think, for Nathan, the idea that this was how his mind worked and that he was stuck with it for the rest of his life was a terrible concept. Unfortunately, his "existential thoughts" became intolerable.

What really killed Nathan? Today my answer starts with depression. Depression is a terrible disease, every bit of a physical entity as pneumonia, diabetes, and cancer. There were chemical reactions in Nathan's brain causing this depression, and neither he nor I could change that.

Depression is exceptionally common; a major depressive episode will occur in 14 percent of adolescents each year[1]. Suicide, unfortunately, is far too often a consequence. It is the second leading cause of death in teenagers (behind accidents—typically car)[2]. Suicide rates have been dramatically increasing in recent years. In 2018, 2,824 teenagers (48,344 people total) died in the U.S. from suicide[3]. In our modest city of Charlotte (population 800,000), about five teenagers die each year by suicide[4]. Across the state, rates of suicide in teenagers have doubled in the last decade and are now at an all-time high.

Yet, depression is very much treatable. With about twenty-nine million teenagers in the U.S.[5], each year about 4.1 million will become depressed (14 percent). With 2,824 dying by suicide, the mortality rate of depression among teenagers is then 0.07%. Suicide is certainly not an inevitable consequence of depression. We can do better. Just as depression is treatable, suicide is no accident. We must work to improve these numbers.

As a pediatrician and parent, 2,824 dying children is not acceptable. Like smoking and obesity, we are going to have to learn to alleviate depression and suicide in our society. Nearly all of us will be affected by one or the other in our lifetimes. If our awareness increases, and our attitudes around mental illness change, we can deal with these issues much more effectively.

1. Substance Abuse and Mental Health Services Administration, *2018 National Survey on Drug Use and Health*, p. 45.

2. Center for Disease Control—Wonder, wonder.cdc.gov.

3. Center for Disease Control—Wonder, wonder.cdc.gov.

4. North Carolina State Center for Health Statistics, https://schs.dph.ncdhhs.gov.

5. US Census Bureau, www.census.gov.

Now that I am part of this community—having lost a child to suicide—it is heart-breaking. At every age from the teen years on, good, brilliant people have succumbed.

My heart aches because despite what the mental health experts told us, Nathan was depressed. We all should have recognized this.

There are many eloquent books written on the psychological agony of major depression. It has been described as feelings of worthlessness, hopelessness, numbness, loneliness, and torture.

Danny Baker from the HuffPost[6] reported that people with depression describe it as a "cancer of the soul" and "a total loss of who you are." Depression "is like drowning, except you can see everyone around you breathing. It feels like falling down a dark bottomless shaft, wondering if and when your fall will ever be caught. And as you look back to where you fell from—which is where you know you need to get back to—you can see it receding further into the distance, the proverbial light becoming dimmer and dimmer, while the shaft into which you are falling becomes deeper, darker, and all the more enveloping."

Nathan once told me the voices in his head "tormented" him. I didn't understand the depths of despair he was describing, or take those comments nearly serious enough. Even as a doctor, I just could not imagine such a thing was ever possible.

Depression is a disease. Medically, we understand it as a physical imbalance of the levels of serotonin in the brain. This is the hormone that controls our feelings of joy, and subsequently, of sadness. In someone with depression, the levels of serotonin are much lower than in other people.

Of course, we cannot measure these levels practically (this is happening in the brain, not the blood), but the physiology is occurring, nonetheless. What triggers the downward spiral into depression and low serotonin levels is complicated. Medially, we might say that depression's cause is iatrogenic (no known specific

---

6. Baker, Danny, *Huffpost Blog*—"*50 Sufferers Describe Depression For People Who've Never Been Depressed*", 7/5/14.

cause) and multifactorial (that many factors come together at once to cause a specific result).

There is evidence of many contributors. Genetics play an important role, as children of depressed adults are more likely to be depressed. If there is a family history of suicide, then that risk increases further. Genetic studies and physical imaging of the brain also show differences between those who are and are not depressed.

One's environment can also have a profound effect. Stress plays an important role physically (on influencing hormones), as well as mentally.

Children who are subject to abuse, trauma, parental divorce, family conflict, and low socioeconomic status are all at increased risk for depression. The most recent research focuses on these Adverse Childhood Experiences (or ACE's).

This research is only beginning, but shows that those growing up in a traumatic environment have an increased risk for not just depression and suicide, but also injury, substance abuse, sexually transmitted diseases, teen pregnancy, cancer, diabetes, and heart disease. ACE's have lasting effects for the rest of one's life.

Chronic medical problems as well as other mental health illness (such as anxiety, substance abuse, and conduct disorders) increase one's risk for developing depression. Previous suicidal attempts and access to firearms have been proven to increase risk as well.

Once one becomes clinically depressed, typical signs may predominate. They may seem obvious, but include feelings of guilt or worthlessness, lack of energy, poor concentration, eating too much or too little, and increased or decreased sleep. In a teenager, this may manifest as mood swings, impulsivity, substance use, poor grades, and poor relationships with parents and peers.

Many of these behaviors seem normal for teenagers. Certainly, Nathan's counselors thought he was a typical teenager. We were persuaded along those lines too. The difference is often an ambiguous level of intensity and duration. The more intense and long these symptoms last, the more likely one is becoming clinically depressed.

Professionally, I often tell parents and patients that when one's mood or mental state begins to interfere with one's daily activities (missing school, affecting relationships with friends and family, or predominating one's personality), then it is a problem.

Oh, how I wish we could have been more perceptive with Nathan.

In May, as the school year ended, we thought Nathan was doing well. We were wrong. I found Nathan one night somewhat catatonic on his bedroom floor. Evidently, he had been laying there for a couple hours, curled up in a ball. I laid down and spooned him. Hugging him seemed to be the only thing I could offer at that moment. Eventually he told me he was lost in his thoughts, and "these thoughts torment me." It was painful and gut-wrenching to speak to him and hear of his agony. My heart ached for him.

This time we brought him to a different psychologist and a psychiatrist as well. After another month, though, both had again reassured us that he was fine. He was discharged from the psychologist's care.

He was evidently not getting any sleep at the time, so the psychiatrist placed him on sleeping pills. "Lack of sleep can make you crazy, so let's see how he does if we can get him to sleep," the psychiatrist told us.

I felt so grateful to that doctor at the time—for Nathan's life was in his hands, and he seemed to have all the answers. Even as a doctor myself, I was beginning to feel at the mercy of Nathan's disease and this doctor's care.

Giving Nathan some rest seemed to help, and within a month Nathan was discharged by him too. The new psychologist and psychiatrist both reassured us that he was fine. We did not have an exit interview with the psychologist this time (indeed we never met with him), but as the psychiatrist let us go, he asked us to check in again in three months only if we had any concerns. It seemed neither of them had any specific concerns of their own.

Looking back on the psychiatrist's notes today, I see that he had diagnosed Nathan with depression, though we did not know this at the time. Evidently, he did not feel any treatment was needed, and he confidentially set Nathan free from his care.

Eerily, I see also in his notes Nathan's words that he would never commit suicide as he "would never want to do that to his family." In Nathan's mind, however, I think these "normal" thoughts were becoming unbearable, even as he failed to understand that or express it to anyone.

Nathan, I think, did have a short respite from his depression that summer. After reassurances from him that he was fine, he went on a pilgrimage with his classmates from our church. This was not meant as a service-oriented trip, but rather as a time to explore and grow one's faith in the company of peers. Nathan was somewhat unsure of going, but we made him.

When he returned, he was beaming from his experiences. He seemed happy with the possibilities of communing with others. On the trip, each teen wrote a letter to himself to be opened three months later. Nathan never got to open his letter, but his leader— our priest—read it at his funeral.

Nathan wrote, "I have had a hard time dealing with a lot of things recently and have been searching for help. The best help I have received is with us [himself]. The pilgrimage we [he and himself] just took has taught us to not overthink and just let the words come out. I hope that you have stuck with this, because it has made the later parts of this week so much easier. You were able to talk and continue a conversation without using your brain. Remember that . . . . I hope you are truly happy and at peace because I am at this moment."

That last line haunts me given Nathan's place today.

Two weeks after his pilgrimage in June, we took a family trip to a dude ranch in Wyoming. It was a wonderful and awe-inspiring trip for all of us, except Nathan. He found no joy in horseback riding or fly fishing. At night he would show up to play cards with the other kids, and he'd light up the room. The little kids would gravitate to him, and he'd bring joy to others.

I now wonder how he felt. I don't really think he felt that joy. Another quote comes to mind from those depressed souls on

HuffPost[7]: "Depression makes you feel like you're an actor playing you—one that's always forced to smile." Or, "It's like mourning the death of someone you once loved—you. When you look in the mirror you see only dead eyes. There is no spark. No joy. No hope. You wonder how you will manage to exist another day."

I cringe now to think this is what Nathan was likely experiencing. These days, I am deeply sympathetic to Nathan and terribly sad that he suffered. I take his final act as a measure of how profoundly terrible depression and mental anguish can be. And I am horrified that he chose to go through it alone.

Unfortunately, not only were we unaware of all that was going on in Nathan's mind, but we had no idea how to help him either. The treatment of depression should be straightforward and effective. Unfortunately, we got it all wrong.

> **Question:** Do you know anyone who is depressed? What made them depressed (genetics, environment, personality)? What helped them recover (themselves, others, therapy, medication)?
>
> **Action:** Make a habit of doing a "Check-up from the Neck-up" with your children (or those you live with). Start at as young an age as possible (children start talking at two years old). Ask about how they are feeling. Ask what makes them feel that way. Tell them how you feel, and how you handle it.

---

7. Baker, Danny, *Huffpost Blog*—*"50 Sufferers Describe Depression For People Who've Never Been Depressed"*, 7/5/14.

5

Inadequate Care

At Nathan's original high school, he was the second of three students to attend there who had died by suicide in a period of three years. After these tragedies, the school invited a couple of psychologists to address the students and parents who were so anxious about this clustering.

The psychologists talked about bullying and its harmful effects, as well as the pitfalls of social media and the effects on the psyche of our teenagers. We were encouraged to speak to our children about suicide and address these issues openly and honestly. I also remember it being brought up to help your teenager to find their "passion" and engage in activities that make them happy. The idea implied seemed to be that these measures could prevent any tragedies.

I have no doubt—as a parent and a pediatrician—that these are important beginnings for dealing with what seems to be a mental health crisis across our nation. However, I can remember sitting in that meeting and listening to the psychologists and checking off all the boxes regarding Nathan, and still being at a loss as to how he died. He was not bullied, he was not on social media much (and not at all the week before his death), he had good friends, and we spoke to him as parents about all these things.

We also tried with Nathan to find his passion, wording that reminded me all too much of the language that was used in developing a college application. Unfortunately, the more Nathan heard this, the more—I believe—he got discouraged. He had all this going for him, yet he could not find a passion, a purpose, or joy. I think this only magnified his depression and hopelessness.

In medical school and my psychiatry rotations, we were taught to address depression and suicide head on. They say to always ask someone who is depressed, "Are you suicidal?" If they tell you they are, you can establish a verbal agreement that they will not follow through on these thoughts. Evidently, you are not going to introduce any ideas that are not already there, and you can help prevent these thoughts from escalating by establishing that contract with the patient.

The implication is that if someone is suicidal, they will tell you. And, if they tell you they are suicidal, you can work through this verbally and prevent any tragedies. This is a good start, but just a start to important work that lies ahead.

As a pediatrician, I care for many patients who struggle through adolescence and become depressed during this time. I still address them as I did Nathan: "Are you depressed?" and "Are you suicidal?" Just because these approaches did not work for Nathan does not mean they cannot help others in the same mental state.

I speak to them with their parents in the room to hopefully encourage and open those avenues of communication. I tell my patients that depression is a physical disease, that it is not their fault, and that it can be devastating for no rhyme or reason. Their willingness to open up and courageously share their pain is critical to relieving that pain.

I offer them hope for the future, remind them that we can treat this, and they will get better with time.

I let them know it is okay not to be passionate about anything, or not to excel at anything. I remind them that it is normal to struggle, and that many college students still do not know what they want to do in life. Most adults will change jobs countless times before, if ever, settling on something they love.

I let them know that even as adults we go through mid-life crises and are unsettled about our purpose in life. I try to take the pressure off them to succeed immediately. I think these new ideas come from sympathy for them, but also because I know all too well that life is often full of struggles. Rather than hopelessness, I try to get them to focus on resilience, persistence, perseverance, and patience.

Life, and especially adolescence, is a rollercoaster. There are valleys to work through. However, by definition, there will be peaks to follow. Just as What goes up must come down, so too, What goes down will eventually come up.

When patients come to me with their mental health problems now, I think how ironically stupid this seems. I often ask them and their parents, "Do you know my story?" In doing so, I'm often thinking to myself, *You know then that I do not have all the answers! In fact, do you really think that I have any answers?*

I'm not sure why they still come to me, but I can think of several of my patients who may have been helped through my experiences.

One such boy was spiraling downward at the time of Nathan's death. I had met with the mother and child several times, and we had been unsuccessful in helping him with his struggles. His frustration and anger were becoming more apparent, and the mom and I both feared his depression was as well. I did not get a chance to see them when Nathan died, but Nathan's death, which was covered in the media, opened the mom's eyes to the gravity of her own son's circumstances.

Shortly thereafter, the boy was enrolled in an inpatient counseling facility. He was away from home for four months, and his way was certainly not easy. However, with his mom's determination to do whatever it took to help her son, he is in a much better place now. I am so thankful that she was willing to become more aggressive and diligent in caring for her son after Nathan's death. I know his death sparked her desperate but successful actions.

I can only hope my story pushes many parents to be diligent in guarding their children's lives. They often spend sleepless nights at home, frustrating time in the Emergency Room, and fearful time in our hospital wards. In the end, it is worth it to preserve their precious child's life.

Perhaps that is why parents still bring me their depressed children. If anything, I can sympathize with them. I understand their pain. I recognize the vital importance of addressing their child's needs. I can completely relate to their incredible love for their children. And I can remind them of the importance of doing anything to keep them safe and healthy.

I can remind my patients of Nathan. I am the face of the miserable parent that they leave behind. I can remind them that there are countless people around them who love them. I tell them that we all will do anything we can to make them better as soon as possible, and that they should not ever feel like they need to go through this alone. I encourage them to speak openly and honestly with their parents, and I encourage the parents to be diligent in their actions.

Our love for our children, open and honest communication with them, and our parental instincts are most important in identifying depression.

I can also reinforce the notion that depression is a treatable disease. Treatment is not only possible but probable.

Two things have been proven to provide effective treatment: therapy and medication. The best therapy for depression is called Cognitive-Behavioral Therapy (or CBT). CBT focuses on acknowledging one's thoughts, feelings, and behaviors. Once identified, a counselor helps the patient reframe those negative thoughts into healthier, happier ones.

Perhaps this is what the lecturers were trying to help us with when they instructed us to "find our child's passion." It sounds simple enough. The key to not being sad is to "find your happy place." Of course, it is not so simple. It takes time, patience, resilience, and persistence. It takes the efforts of a trained counselor, a willing patient, and a supportive community.

I believe family therapy is vital to this treatment as well (though it has not been proven to be effective alone). It is critical for parents to be involved and experience this with their children. Open communication and conflict resolution are important means to maintain mental health within the family, and parents should insist on being part of their children's therapy. Both personally and professionally, I find this aspect lacking far too often.

In the teenage years, the most common medications used for the treatment of depression are SSRI's or Selective Serotonin Reuptake Inhibitors. Prozac is perhaps the most well-known example, but there are many safe alternatives in this class of medication. They are "selective" in that they specifically attack what is physically lacking in the depressed patient's brain: Serotonin. As such, they are effective and safe.

Unfortunately, they often take six to eight weeks to achieve their maximum effectiveness (though some benefit may be noticed as early as two weeks). This can be an agonizing—but necessary— wait for relief from one's depression and is another reason therapy and medication should be used together. Therapy and medication have both been shown to work for depression, but they are most effective when used together.

For me, this symbiotic benefit is so important that if a patient is on antidepressant medication, I insist he or she is also engaging in therapy.

If depression is such a terrible disease, why then are we so reluctant to deal with it as such? In Nathan's case, we were encouraged by his psychologist not to mention his mental struggles when applying to his new high school. After consulting with Nathan, we did not bring it up to the priests who accompanied him on his pilgrimage that summer. His friends and teachers knew nothing of his struggles. The school knew he had a concussion, and they dealt with that appropriately. But there was no mention of depression in any of these public arenas.

In society, our problems along these lines seem even worse. We think of depression as a sign of weakness. We lack sympathy for the mentally ill, and often blame them for their own troubles. We think it is their own fault, and they should be the ones to pull themselves out of their own hole.

As a pediatrician, I refer my patients to specialists of all kinds. Most of the time, I get those doctors' notes, not only to keep me generally abreast of how they are treating any complex issues, but also to make me aware so that I too can keep an eye on things and assist in their care along the way. These notes and communication are an important way to organize and coordinate a person's care. The only doctors who routinely do not send me their notes are psychologists and psychiatrists.

Uniformly, I think they are so stuck in some detrimental idea of privatization of patients' records and sensitivity of the issues being discussed at these visits, that they are sacrificing any and all outside help for the patient. My patients often tell me they have signed a request for these doctors to release these records to me—their primary care doctor—yet they still refuse.

After Nathan's death, I approached many professionals searching for ways I could help prevent suicide in others. I actually ran against the most closed minds in the psychological fields. I think sometimes doctors are so accomplished and confident that they feel they know how best to remedy a situation. The psychological leaders I approached demonstrated this idea, and were often unresponsive to any fresh ideas about how to change the system, help their patients, and extend ourselves in new ways to improve patient care.

It is beyond time we change the stigma of depression and mental illness. I envision a future when we rally around a depressed colleague or peer in the same way we support those with cancer, diabetes, or heart disease. For Nathan's sake, I'm a bit envious of the attention cancer gets. Bracelets, ribbons, pink uniforms, and fundraisers are appropriately part of the aggressive ways in which we draw attention to the needs and suffering of these patients. And positive changes in care—and cures—will follow.

Why not address mental illness the same way? How much better off would our depressed friends be if they were wholeheartedly supported by their community? It would be great if we substituted bullying, social media stigmas, and peer pressure with lovingkindness toward those who need it most.

What Nathan did not realize as he suffered alone within his own mind was that he was not alone. Many of us will go through a bout of depression, most of us will have periods of mental illness at some point in our lives, and nearly all of us have someone in our immediate community of friends and family who are suffering in this way. These people need our help as much as anyone.

Nathan spent a lot of time in his room those last months. It seemed reasonable. He had homework, he studied, and presumably communicated with his friends on his cell phone. One thing he did not do, though, was search the Internet. He did not search for help, explore depression, inquire about suicide, or even muddle through songs or ideas about depression.

I'm fearful that in those last months—in all that time in his room, during all those sleepless nights—Nathan was simply lost in his thoughts. And those thoughts—that depression—tormented him.

We did not see this side of Nathan most of the time though. He seemed to have a good summer. I wrote in my journal around this time, "When Nathan is up, he is very happy, loving toward his sister, chatty, and fun to be around. We live for those times!"

We were still worried about him, but it seemed more like normal worrying about a typical teenager. He had football practice and was making new friends. And he enthusiastically played his Xbox with his old friends.

He started at his new school in late August. He glowed after his first day. Teachers actually spoke personally to the students and cared about them. His English class was based on graphic novels. His science teacher blew out a ceiling tile by exploding some gas. And he even got a "shout out" in front of the whole football team for his play at cornerback in their first scrimmage.

Everything appeared headed in the right direction. And then came the concussion.

Question: How aware are you of your feelings? How do you deal with your feelings? Do you ignore them? Let them bottle up inside you? Do you share them with others? Do you take action to deal with them? Do you see a therapist?

Action: Make it a habit to do something each day that brings you joy. Something just for you. My suggestions: enjoy a certain snack or dessert, take a walk, spend time with your pet, talk to someone you care about, hug, or play.

6

Head Trauma

The second football scrimmage was on a Friday night. On Sunday, Nathan approached me and said he had headaches since the game and thought he had a concussion. He could even identify the single play where it happened. He was covering the kickoff. They had a great kicker who always kicked it far in the end zone for a touchback.

As the opposing player took a knee ending the play, Nathan let up. Out of nowhere, another player launched himself into Nathan, helmet-to-helmet, right in his temple, knocking him down. It was alarming, but nothing really out of the ordinary. I certainly remember playing football in high school and taking every opportunity to hit anyone from the other team. We all probably see this "unnecessary roughness" every weekend in the Fall (though such plays are illegal now and can get a player kicked out of the game for "targeting").

It was the type of play we are warned about these days, especially with the increased emphasis on the dangers of concussions. After Nathan complained of those persistent headaches, we brought him to the concussion experts in town. Tests showed he had significantly slowed brain responses, which is a clear sign of a concussion.

What's more, his mood had changed for the worse. His school and doctors were aggressive in caring for Nathan. For two weeks, he stayed home on complete brain rest. He was not allowed to play video games, do homework, or engage in any stimulating activity.

He'd linger for the morning, then take long naps in the afternoon when his headaches returned. He was not allowed on the football field, even to stand on the sideline for fear that he would take an incidental blow. He was isolated. By three weeks, he was back in school, came home, and took those naps. Still no homework. By four weeks, he was doing minimal work and started to catch up on his school work.

At parent night around that time, Sarah and I met with his teachers. Many showed concern for him, recognized that he was still a little "flat" in the classroom, but were also glad to see that he was getting better. Two weeks later, he was caught up with his work and symptom free.

We know much more about concussions these days and certainly respect and care for injuries to the brain better than in the past. A concussion can simply be defined as a traumatic brain injury caused by a blow or jolt to the head. It is diagnosed when any symptoms persist after head trauma.

Those symptoms can be obvious, like loss of consciousness or amnesia, but are far more often subtle. Today, we know that headaches, blurry vision, dizziness, sensitivity to light and noise, and drowsiness or poor sleep are all important signs of a concussion. Mental symptoms are also common and include memory loss, feeling sluggish, foggy, or just not right. Intellectually, one may have difficulty concentrating, a slowed reaction time, and confusion.

Immediately, sports trainers are now taught to be protective of their athletes' brains and be cautious when allowing an athlete to return to play after a blow to the head. On-field assessments are based on the symptoms above, and generally if there are any symptoms or suspicion of a concussion, the athlete is removed from the game and not allowed to return until cleared at a medical doctor's office at a later time.

There are two main reasons for this aggressive approach. First, when one is recovering from a concussion, the risk of additional concussions is great. The next concussion will happen with a lesser blow, and take a longer time to recover from. Repeated concussions often cause prolonged symptoms and not only risk the athlete missing their whole season, but eventually there is a point where the risk of playing again at all has to be considered too great.

The evidence for when to remove a child from playing a certain sport all together is not conclusive yet, and still an art form best discussed with a concussion expert. We regularly hear stories about professional athletes who suffer from these symptoms the rest of their lives.

The other reason to be cautious is called second-impact syndrome and is even more serious. When recovering from a concussion, a second blow can be crippling to the complex bio-chemical recovery going on in the brain. Second-impact syndrome describes sudden death in such a circumstance. Children are particularly susceptible to this calamity.

In light of these effects, the American Medical Association called for a ban of boxing in 1984. (More recently, without a complete ban, they have called for improved safety measures including required headgear. This, too, has not been universally adopted). Knocking someone out in the boxing ring is by definition a concussion, and to continue boxing after this is to risk further, sometimes very serious injury.

CNN reported in 2019 that on average thirteen boxers die in the ring a year. Many more suffer permanent brain damage. The terms "punch drunk syndrome" and "dementia pugilistica" have been part of the medical literature since 1928 and 1937 respectively. Today, we are beginning to describe the chronic effects of concussions on all athletes as "Chronic Traumatic Encephalopathy" or CTE.

Medically, Nathan's concussion was cared for very well, with all the latest research-proven techniques applied. I often describe a concussion to my patients as an injury to the brain, similar to a sprained ankle. No injury is identifiable on a CT scan, but there is certainly damage done.

When a patient sprains an ankle, it takes time to heal. First, we rest the injury until there is no pain. Then we allow the patient to progress with their activities as tolerated without pain. The old adage "If it hurts to walk on the injury, then don't walk on it!" is sound medical advice.

Full speed, competitive activities are last in a line of progression that one can only move through if they are pain free. For if there is pain when you are injured, then that injury is aggravated, and an acute situation can become chronic.

Recovery from a concussion is similar. Of course all activities involve the brain. Even reading, homework, and video games can exacerbate a concussion and severely impact the time it takes to recover. With concussions, one can only move forward with activities when one is symptom free. The progression of activity I typically prescribe for a patient involves first complete rest (naps and quiet dark rooms); light reading and work; limited TV; walking and going to school; light exercise; significant training; and then return to play competitively.

At a minimum, once a person is symptom free at rest, this process takes a week. For Nathan, his recovery lasted six weeks.

Nathan seemed to have recovered by October 4. He was cleared by the concussion specialist that day. We, too, certainly thought he was doing well. We had tried to keep those communication lines open during this trial, and he had always reassured us he was doing fine, sometimes vehemently.

Still, I wish we had paid more attention to his mental state. His history of depression was never discussed at the doctors' offices. In retrospect, he should have at least revisited his psychologist and psychiatrist. Whatever hopeless thoughts that were going on in his head, he kept to himself.

It is all too clear to me now that a history of depression and a patient's mood in general is a critical aspect to evaluating and treating one who has suffered a concussion.

As a teenager, I think his psyche did not allow him to deal with this injury and his depression in a constructive way. It also alienated him from us so that we did not recognize the full effects of Nathan's disease. I am devastated when I realize that in those last months, Nathan suffered mostly alone. Once again, his willingness to share in his pain (or lack thereof) was so important to his full recovery.

The concussion certainly affected Nathan both directly and indirectly. Directly, it gave him daily headaches, slowed his cognition, and depressed his mood. Indirectly, it removed him from everything positive. Nathan seemed to be moving in a good direction at the time of his concussion. He was thrilled with his new school and possibilities for learning, he was working hard and enjoying football, and he seemed complacent with his home life.

His relationship with his friends, however, was not perfect. This was important to Nathan, and I worry that he may have felt lost in this regard. He had left his old friends for reasonable reasons, but did he feel he abandoned them? I am not sure.

At his new school, the concussion seemed to eliminate any possibilities of cultivating new relationships. He was not physically present in school or on the field; when he was there, he was not in any mood to socialize. I'm sure this all affected him deeply.

Furthermore, I wonder if he suffered similarly to someone who has bipolar disorder. For those who suffer from bipolar disorder, they waver between periods of extreme depression and mania. In their depressed state, they may contemplate suicide, but are often too morose to act on these feelings. It is only when they emerge from their depression—in a fit of overactivity, impulsivity, and mania—that they often act on their despair.

It is another terrible mental disease that greatly increases the risk of suicide. Perhaps Nathan's recovery from his concussion was similar. He seemed to have recovered from his concussion, but somehow was left with the will to act on his extremely depressive thoughts.

So what damage to Nathan's brain was left after this "recovery?" It is impossible for me to think of Nathan these days and not also consider CTE. A hot topic at all levels of football, CTE is the damage left to the brain after repetitive concussions, or after even lesser, repetitive blows to the head.

Often the symptoms of such damage are difficulty thinking, emotional instability, impulsivity, depression, and suicidal thoughts. In a recent study of NFL players, 110 of 111 players had evidence of CTE. Tragically, many former players have committed suicide, and a postmortem exam often reveals the effects of CTE. It seems obvious and evident at this point that repeated blows to the head can cause brain damage.

All this is certainly a source of much fear and trepidation among all involved and makes me wonder about Nathan. Nathan grew up playing football and rugby, so he was exposed to head trauma. Nathan suffered one other known concussion at the age of ten. After rest, he played the rest of that football season with a pad over his helmet to help reduce the impact of further blows.

When Nathan died and it became apparent that the state wanted to autopsy his body, I distinctly recall asking twice for them to check him for CTE. In the confusion of that time, however, it was not done. Ultimately, these are now more questions that were left unanswered.

That concussion is now just another factor in an endless string of events that built up to destroy Nathan's mind and body.

Question: How does the importance of head trauma and new research into brain damage affect your views on athletics? Does this view change with the age of the athlete?

Action: List those experiences you've had with concussions (either personally or with teammates)? Was it addressed at the time? Do you know anyone who was affected by a concussion for an extended period of time?

7

A Perfect Storm

How could this have happened? Why did Nathan kill himself? Nathan had every advantage in the world. He was not picked on or bullied. He had good friends and was well liked. He received a lot of love from his family, and he knew it. Yet, he chose to leave all this behind.

It makes no sense to me today, even as a loving parent and physician. Somehow, he could not tolerate to be part of this world any longer. So many of my questions will forever be unanswered.

I often think of the many glorious stories of those who narrowly avoid death through some seemingly divine intervention, a confluence of coincidences that miraculously leads one down a narrow path of survival. Perhaps you've heard stories of a friend who chose not to fly on a particular flight that later crashed; or didn't go to school on the day a shooter showed up; or who just happened to stop their car at a green light as another car sped through the intersection.

When I think of Nathan's downfall over the last months of his life, I can see a bit of the circumstances that led to his overwhelming despair. His demise was a depressing, perfect storm of coincidences that piled up in the wrong direction to beat him down.

I often wish if I had just done something differently—had engaged him one more time, had just told him I loved him once more—maybe I could have saved his life. Could I have stopped this downward spiral at some point? Where was his guardian angel?

Unfortunately, in Nathan's mind there was a rising tide of hopelessness and despair that magnified and erupted uncontrollably. In the end, Nathan was terribly depressed. But what triggered this, and why could we not treat it effectively?

The signs of a concussion and of depression mirror the normal behavior of a teenager. This is no coincidence, as teens are more at risk of suicide (as are those suffering from a concussion). Often, at work, I'd lament with my co-workers how our teenage children were driving us mad. They played too many video games; were too disrespectful; wasted away their days in their rooms; did not socialize enough; and were terribly moody.

In many ways, these three areas are quite similar. But two are disease states, a pathology that can worsen and lead to significant complications. The other, being a teenager, is a normal phase of growing up, developing one's identity and learning to live in the world. Those who make it through the teen years should be more mature, resilient, and have a greater sense of self. Hopefully, they are better people for all the aggravation they go through and cause their parents.

As a pediatrician, when I differentiate normal childhood behaviors from pathologic ones, I often focus on how these behaviors are affecting a child's life. Are they sleeping well? Eating okay? Do they tolerate school? And enjoy their friends? Do they have a healthy self-confidence and self-esteem?

Remember, when childhood aggression and behavior, anxieties and mood begin to interfere with daily routines, it is a problem. A parent's intuition is critical. If you are worried about your child's mental health, you deserve answers. Of course, we missed the subtle clues of Nathan's situation. Furthermore, three mental health experts reassured us of Nathan's well-being.

After his psychology appointments, I'd ask Nathan how it went. His standard reply was "Fine." I'd ask if he wanted to talk about anything that came up. He'd say, "No." I'd push a little further: "Well, the most important thing is to talk through your issues. You need to talk to someone about everything you're going through. Are you comfortable talking to this doctor?" And I would get a simple "Yes." That was it. And it sounded pretty normal to me. Of course, that was months before he died.

Throughout those last months and even closer to his death—when Nathan seemed down—I would ask, "Are you doing okay?" Again, just "Yes." "Are you depressed?" "No." "Do you ever think of hurting yourself, or that you just don't want to be here anymore?" "No!" "You'd tell us if so, right?" "Yes!" End of conversation.

About a month before he died, Sarah asked him about following up with the psychiatrist. He became visibly angry and refused. He did not go back to the psychiatrist. Was that anger a sign of deepening depression? Had he already lost hope? He did not tell anyone that either.

Often I think Nathan's decision to die was quick, urgent, and decisive. Teenagers can be terribly impulsive. This makes me think there was nothing we could have done about his suicide. Of course, that is not good enough. Especially if the same issues are popping up with your teenager.

Suicide is not an inevitable result of a depressed teenager! It should never be considered a quick solution to an overwhelming problem. Quite the opposite: With direct attention by all, it can be avoided.

If I were to list those aggravating facts that magnified catastrophically into Nathan's suicide, the list would sound manageable. Intelligent. Sensitive. Passionate. Teenager. Depression. Concussion. Poor advice. No answers.

Maybe there were also more insidious forces at work. Silence. Non-helicopter parents. Independence. Determination. Perfectionist. Foolishness (Nathan did not have to face his fears alone).

As his parent, I wish we could have addressed Nathan's needs more effectively. It is not that I think we didn't love Nathan, or do our best to support and care for him. But the fact is that this world failed him, and we were the biggest part of his world.

Sarah and I reached out to Nathan numerous times over those last months. When he suffered the concussion, she asked him several times if he wanted to go back to the psychiatrist. She finally quit asking when he aggressively refused. I questioned Nathan about suicidal thoughts right up to his death. He always vehemently denied such thoughts. We discussed depression too. I tried to instill a sense of peace in his restless mind.

We offered to bring him to youth group, to rejoin those friends from the pilgrimage. We explored activities he may like, including trying to discover his "passion." I now wonder if these efforts—and his failure to respond to them—just made him feel more worthless. I think that he felt, with all the opportunities he had, if he could not be happy under these circumstances, then maybe he was the problem.

We spoke about Nathan's worth as a human being in the eyes of God and that God was willing to sacrifice his own son for Nathan. I prayed for Nathan directly, especially during those times his struggles came to a head. I prayed privately for God to give me the ability to exemplify his light and love to Nathan. And I prayed for Nathan to recognize this and accept it for himself.

When Nathan continued to struggle, I expressed my concerns over his soul and my inability to bring him peace through my prayers. I recognized that only God could deliver this blessing, and so I specifically handed Nathan over to God. I asked God to save Nathan where I could not. I worry now that I was just passively letting Nathan go and not working as hard as I should have to reach him.

As much as I loved Nathan, I most often wish I had been more diligent in my love and care for him. In the end, did we let our guard down and let Nathan slip through our fingers?

In pediatrics, "helicopter" parents have a bad reputation of suffocating their children's independence and limiting their creativity and resiliency. Though it is not in my nature, I wish with all my heart that I had helicoptered over Nathan. The only reason I don't feel completely guilty about Nathan's death is I know I gave him all the love I had. Yet I still wish I had given him more.

If only I had visited him in his room one more time, sat down and talked with him more, pried out his feelings, or tried to understand them just a bit more. Would that have made a difference? I'll never know the answer to that now. All the questions of this world are left unanswered. It is all as confusing to me today as it was that day he left our house forever.

I can list all the areas that we fell short in addressing Nathan's needs. That list starts with Nathan not opening up about his feelings. Perhaps we should have done a better job modeling this behavior. We could have more regularly and much earlier spoken about such things as a family.

I would be more demanding of Nathan's mental health professionals. I would have insisted that Sarah and I were a more deliberate part of his care. I would have integrated "family therapy" into his individual therapy, encouraging us all to open up with each other with the therapist present. I would have continued to love Nathan, making him aware of this in bad times as well as good.

At times when I was most frustrated with him, I would better tolerate his shortcomings, remind myself of my graceful love for him, and I would have told him this (again and again). I would have tried harder to engage him in activities with us (to find things he enjoyed doing) without putting pressure on him to be engaged or happy.

I would have hugged him more. I would have met him in his own territory more often. I would have sat in his room with him weekly—even daily—to observe and discuss how he was doing. I would have sympathized with him openly, cared for him physically, and prayed that he would let me cry with him. I would have told him one more time—if not one hundred times—that I loved him.

Today, all I can do is pass on these lessons to my other children. And encourage you to focus on these issues and be aggressively diligent with your love for your children.

I now know where the expression "having a hole in your heart" comes from. I always understood the symbolism, but when Nathan died I felt as though there was a large, empty cavity in my chest. I could literally feel the darkness and void. It was difficult to breathe. I was numb. The four days without knowing were terrible. But now our lives will never be the same. That emptiness will always be there.

Sarah and I have twice visited the site where Nathan died. Immediately afterward, the local police and the mushroom collector who found Nathan took us to the spot. We laid flowers, said a prayer, and said goodbye to our son for the hundredth time that week. We gave the mushroom collector the reward for finding our son, and a hug for answering our prayers in bringing Nathan home to us.

We also visited that site on the one-year anniversary of Nathan's death. By then the mushroom collector had constructed a cross of rocks on the ground below where Nathan would have hung. Our dried flowers were embedded among the rocks.

We took a picture of the cross, and then Sarah turned her camera up at the tree canopy above. Somehow, the light breaking through the leaves made the perfect image of an angel. Wings widespread, it floated peacefully with the breeze.

The tree itself was decomposing. I wrote at the time: "When you look up, you can see the tree on which Nathan died. It is now broken in half and quickly rotting to nothing. Almost as if God has destroyed it in his anger and sadness over the tragedy of Nathan's mental illness, much like he tore the veil of the temple in half and shook the earth when Jesus died."

But that was a year later. Where was God when Nathan was suffering? Why could not God have shown up more deliberately and helpfully earlier? Why could he not have at least guided me or Sarah or the psychiatrist to ease his pain? Why all this suffering in the first place? With a loving God, why does death exist at all?

Our answers began with a song.

Question: What times did it seem like all life's events where stacked against you? What or who are those most solid foundations you turn to when the whole world is against you? Who or what can you really count on in this life?

Action: Start a journal. In your journal, include the mental, emotional, and spiritual events of your day. Recognize or comment on the unstable nature of these aspects of your psyche. Begin to discern how you can anticipate and modify the low times.

8

Spiritual Verse

On October 13, 2017, we had been searching for Nathan for four days. I had not slept more than two or three hours a night. I'd lost ten pounds. And had driven frantically all over investigating new, ultimately fruitless ideas about where Nathan was.

The police were also searching our area. Bulletins had been distributed. A reward was offered. The Internet was abuzz with friends' pleas for help. Monks were praying for him in New England. Candles were lit in California. Two separate private detectives had been searching for clues all week. And the FBI was looking beyond our state.

Then the chief detective called our home. He wanted to know if Sarah and I were home so he could stop by. I'm not even sure if we had met him personally at that point.

And so we sat there anxiously awaiting his arrival, afraid of what that meant. Four people arrived, including one of our independent private investigators. As we sat down, there was no way around the news: "We found your son hanging from a tree."

Sarah and I were on the couch. She cried. I got down on my knees and hugged her. Our nightmarish week had turned into a permanent reality. We would never wake up from this darkness.

Quickly, Taber came down to hear that his brother was not coming home. Someone was sent to get Elle Louise before social media notified her. Two priests from our church showed up, and I went with one to get my mother. All she could say was "Oh, Jonathan. You do not deserve this! Oh, Nathan!"

Sure enough, by the time we returned home, newscasters who had interviewed us during the search for Nathan were already alerting us to the fact that his discovery was being broadcast on their networks. Someone, somewhere had intercepted the police scanners.

I remember wanting to see Nathan. "I just want to hug my son one last time!"

Days later, I found out why I was not allowed to see him when I read the coroner's report. Apparently, much decomposition happens in just four days, especially when out in the wilderness. His body was unidentifiable.

The coroner eventually matched Nathan's dental records to confirm it was him, but we already knew. The police suspected it was him as they found his car in the nearby parking lot. He had walked about a half mile into the woods until he found a large, fallen tree that was suspended just the right distance above the ground.

For us, only one thing confirmed that it was Nathan they found that Friday night in 2017. It was the shirt he was wearing. When the police asked for a description of Nathan, we gave them the most recent pictures we had. More importantly, though, Sarah had seen him briefly in the hallway before he left. She told them he was definitely wearing his green Led Zeppelin t-shirt.

It had a yellow outline of the Led Zeppelin angel on it. We thought of it as his "Stairway to Heaven" shirt (Led Zeppelin's most famous song). Perhaps Nathan thought this, too, for the only thing he did before leaving our house on that fateful day was change out of his pajamas into that shirt.

Whether it was Nathan's intent or God using this "coincidence" to calm our souls, that shirt sent us a powerful message. We really didn't contemplate the song much during Nathan's disappearance, but after learning of his death, we poured over its lyrics for answers.

Through that shirt, we were drawn to that song, and every word seemed to give us more of an understanding of what Nathan had been through and was continuing to experience. And so, our first answers were a spiritual message delivered in the form of a hard rock anthem.

Led Zeppelin was a wild, hard rock band of the seventies, the epitome of sex, drugs, and rock and roll. Their music was loud and the group themselves, especially the lead guitarist, Jimmy Page, was mesmerized by the occult. When "Stairway to Heaven" was released, the rumor was if you played the record backwards, you could hear, "Here's to my sweet Satan."

An image of an angel based on an eighteenth century painting became one of their primary symbols. The angel is in agony, reaching up to heaven while one toe dips down onto earth. One theory is that it is a depiction of Satan. Sarah and I actually visited that original painting where it was on display in Boston. It has a completely different meaning for us.

God has a way of using the worst tragedies on this earth for his own purposes. The ultimate example of this is Jesus' horrific death by crucifixion. That shadow of Good Friday has been replaced by the glory of Easter. Even the cross itself, once a symbol of torture, intimidation, and death is now a glorious sign of the grace and salvation Jesus provides through his sacrifice.

For Sarah and me, after learning of Nathan's death, the song "Stairway to Heaven" and the image of that fallen angel became a light from God. When I see that angel today, I see Nathan. Although he is clearly distressed—the pain of depression etched on his face—he is also gifted with wings and a halo. He is saved from his torment.

In lieu of a suicide note, the song itself has been transformed into God's message for us. It fully describes Nathan's last months on earth, his struggles with depression, God's call to him, Nathan's answer, and ultimately his security and salvation in heaven.

As Sarah and I absorbed the news of Nathan's death and began to plan his funeral, it became increasingly important to us that we use this song in his service. This was not without controversy, though, as there were some conflicting ideas among our clergy about its appropriateness.

Even now, I have not been granted permission by Led Zeppelin to use their lyrics for this book. They gave no answer, but evidently our interpretation is too controversial for them as well.

As I prayed for guidance before the funeral, God's answer came to me from the song itself. As is stated in the second stanza, sometimes words do have more than one meaning. For me, these words now signal the beginning of my healing and spiritual transformation after Nathan's death. No matter what the song's original purpose was or how the band prefers it be seen today, through God, this song now gives me hope.

In the end, Sarah read the lyrics of "Stairway to Heaven" at Nathan's funeral as part of his eulogy. She read it, substituting the word "Lad" (Nathan) for "Lady," and "God" for "Gold" (a traditional symbol for God). The "Piper" of the song is God, calling us all to join him.

Though I cannot print these lyrics, I invite you to search for them, write them in the margins if you like, and recognize the infinite beauty we see in their message. Every word in its specific relation to Nathan's story comforts us with the knowledge that God understands what he went through. Hopefully, its poetic message will have meaning to you, too, as it reminds us all of the peace and comfort we can share with Nathan in the future.

As depicted in the beginning of this song, Nathan struggled with his religion. Even so, it seems the most meaningful and enjoyable time he had during those months prior to his death was the pilgrimage he took with the youth at our church. It was meant as a spiritual journey, a chance to explore one's faith among peers, and to grow in the process. Recall the letter he wrote to himself during that trip.

Nathan gives his perspective on his depression: "I have been having a hard time dealing with a lot of things recently and have been searching for help. The best help I have received is with us [himself]."

Nathan at first tried to work his own way out of his depression and toward his salvation.

In that letter, he also seems more focused on his mood and the friendships he made than his relationship with God.

These methods failed him. Yet, despite this failure, he knew if he just asked God for forgiveness and handed his life over to him, he would be saved. Unfortunately, Nathan's impulsive, teenage mind misguided him even in light of this profound truth.

Still, Romans 10:9 speaks to all of us, "If you confess with your mouth Jesus as Lord and believe in your heart that God raised him from the dead, you will be saved."

Jesus, while being crucified, reached out to the criminals on either side of him, moments before their deaths. And when one of them responded kindly, Jesus told him (Luke 23:43), "Truly I say to you, today you shall be with Me in Paradise."

One word, can make all the difference.

It is terribly painful for me to admit that this earth failed Nathan, and we were all part of that. Not through lack of effort or love; but through our own imperfections, we were unable to save Nathan. If we try to buy our way to heaven through deeds and actions, we will not succeed. Only in word, in humbly turning ourselves over to God's grace, can we be saved.

Nathan's plight is a sad physical and spiritual reminder of this truth so beautifully stated in the first stanza of "Stairway to Heaven." To be sure, as becomes clear as this poem progresses, Nathan was saved on that fateful day.

The song itself alludes to the duel meanings it presents in the second stanza. I use it now as a story of hope, love, and grace. God presented it to Sarah and me this way, and we heard. Hopefully, my use of this message to spread God's word, to enlighten others to our knowledge, and to turn others toward God and strengthen their faith is proof enough of the goodness it represents.

It becomes a self-fulfilling prophecy that in using these words for good, they become good. It is up to each of us, though, to hear these lyrics in our own way, and hopefully recognize God's purposes. In doing so, we can spread that light, and Satan's effects— the evil in this world—will take a little less hold.

With God's help, I will do my best to relate this message to you. It is up to you to hear that message and use it to strengthen your own relationship with God.

As the song moves on and describes the feelings of loss, it takes me to the story of Lazarus, a foreshadowing resurrection just before Jesus is to meet his fate. Mary and Martha's brother is ill and soon to die, yet Jesus' first response to their plea for him to come help is this, "This sickness is not to end in death, but for the glory of God, so that the Son of God may be glorified by it" (John 11:4).

By the time Jesus arrives, Lazarus has been dead and entombed for four days (Nathan was found four days after killing himself). Mary and Martha's responses to Jesus' arrival differ in many ways, but they both greet him with the same frustrated (perhaps even angry) statement, "Lord, if You had been here, my brother would not have died" (John 11:21, 32). Well before Nathan's death—as he struggled—I prayed many times that God would save him. Yet he died. God seemingly showed up too late. Like Mary and Martha, I wish God would have arrived just a bit sooner.

Jesus' response to all of us is this, "I am the resurrection and the life; he who believes in Me will live even if he dies, and everyone who lives and believes in Me will never die" (John 11:25–26). Indeed, we all will meet our physical death, but it is by God's grace and Jesus' sacrifice that we are yet able to live. No time is too late to recognize this.

These stanzas and the story of Lazarus to me are as much about the agony of death as the glory of resurrection. Led Zeppelin perfectly describes my feelings of remorse in these days as full of misgiving thoughts and a crying spirit.

John relays Jesus' emotions as he arrives to find the town mourning Lazarus' death, "When Jesus therefore saw her weeping, and the Jews who came with her also weeping, He was deeply moved in spirit and was troubled" (John 11:33).

Even though he knows he is about to wipe away all their tears with Lazarus' resurrection, "Jesus wept" (John 11:35). Jesus (and God) weeps alongside us, even in heaven, as the struggles of life seemingly consume us.

In Nathan's case, we found him in a tree in a forest (no brook). Our feelings are as mixed and complicated as Nathan's. As much as we still hold fast to God's salvation and peace, the torment of Nathan's leaving still haunts us. Our family's spirit is crushed. We have cried, mourned, and also stood bewildered. There is still so much ambiguity around his death.

Why did Nathan die? Where did his good deeds get him? His kind thoughts, his brilliant mind, his gifted fortunes . . . what good were they? Our own faith and prayers did not seem to help.

These mind-boggling questions can also be posed to loved ones randomly affected by cancer, the latest school shootings, the many injustices of this world and, for that matter, any untimely death. This earth's ways are cloudy. Truth and purpose are often obscured by "smoke," and we are left standing, looking on with uncertainty.

On earth, there are many evils and circumstances that affect us deeply, yet are beyond our control. God gives us free will on earth, but we often abuse it, beginning with the original sin. We are often terribly influenced by those imperfections within ourselves and others, and those random imperfections of the earth. Sin, sadness, and death come to us all ultimately. At this point, all I can do is look to the only positive certainty I have—God's world—and his place in ours.

I frequently have told others that as much as we are sure of Nathan's spiritual message and salvation, we are puzzled by his story on earth. Roles seem reversed for us now. The physical nature of this world is clouded. Our only certainty is our faith and God's ultimate love for us all. In fact, I don't describe it as my faith anymore; it is this knowledge to which I cling. My spirit is crying out, but the only real security I have now is not of this world but in the next.

The song now turns to us all and to you specifically. What place does Nathan's story have in your life, and what place do you have on this earth? God reaches out to us all, sometimes in a whisper, sometimes loud and clear, but always he does. Your place, then, is to humbly listen, hear, and act on this message. If you contemplate Nathan's journey and the meaning of your life, then I believe you will reasonably find your way to God.

Then in handing over your life to God and proclaiming your faith in him and your salvation through Jesus, God will lead you, and a new day will dawn. Ultimately, all the evils and death on this earth are mere shadows . . . temporary hurdles, hopefully leading us closer to our Savior, so that the light of a new day can radiantly overcome them. In the end, as we fall into God's embrace, peace and joy will reign.

In Nathan's case, I can only imagine how desperate and depressed he must have been during those last months. Hopefully none of us ever come to understand the depths of depression that lead people to kill themselves. I suppose the killing itself begins to relay how deep that despair must be. Either way, God cleaned his spring soul. As the song eludes, Nathan was born in May.

Nathan had moments of despair prior to his death, and I prayed for him often. When we couldn't find him for four days in February, I certainly prayed even more to God that this was his means of reaching Nathan's soul. I prayed that as great as his torment was, was how great this trial needed to be to turn his heart and soul to God.

Nathan was certainly headed down a deep, dark path with his depression, but there is always a way out in the Lord. There was always time to change the direction he was headed. My hope was that God was working on Nathan, touching his soul, and saving him. I think God ultimately did that, but not at all in the ways I had hoped. Ultimately, Nathan was cleansed, restored, and reborn. It is all any of us can hope for.

Over the last three months of Nathan's life, he actually seemed to be doing just fine and happy more often than not. He suffered that concussion, but was recovering from that too ("95% better" in his own words). At that point, I had nearly forgotten the two breakdowns he had had earlier that year.

Six months prior to his death, Nathan had run away for three hours. He was frustrated with school and his place in this world. Three months later, I found him on the floor in his room, almost catatonic. That was when he told me, "I'm tormented by my thoughts."

Both times, we brought Nathan to see a psychologist. They both convinced us he was a normal teenager, impulsive and analytical, but fine.

When I get to the second to last verse of "Stairway to Heaven," I get chills down my spine, and my heart freezes. It is still the most eloquent, profound, and saddest account of Nathan's situation to me. It becomes so clear to me what Nathan was going through all along, and I cannot believe I largely ignored it at the time.

Nathan's head was truly humming in ways he did not understand, he could not control; in so many ways, it scared and "tormented" him. In the end, I think it was the fear of living life like this forever that led him to the conclusion that there was no other way out than suicide.

Was God calling Nathan to join him? Certainly not in a literal, immediate way. God does not wish this level of torment on anyone. He is always calling out to us though. Isaiah (43:1) speaks to this: "But now, thus says the Lord, your Creator, O Jacob, And He who formed you, O Israel, 'Do not fear, for I have redeemed you; I have called you by name, you are Mine!'"

Specifically, that person in the Trinity down here on earth—the Holy Spirit—achingly desires to be with you. James 4:5 describes it thus, "He jealously desires the Spirit which he has made to dwell in us."

An examination of the Greek word used in this verse offers a better interpretation. *Epipotheo* is a juxtaposition of the words *epi* ("over") and *potheo* ("desire"). Together they describe an intense desire, a yearning, an aching hunger. They also describe the quality of the desire our God, the Spirit, the Piper, has for each one of us.

I think in Nathan's desperation and hopelessness (interpreted by his immature, adolescent brain), he misinterpreted the immediacy and means with which to join God. But I think Nathan heard that calling, and I think this verse perfectly describes Nathan's state of mind at the time of his death. The verse does not end there though.

My father died three years prior to Nathan. His death from cancer was sudden and unexpected (he died a month after being diagnosed). It was gut wrenching for my mother, my brother, and me. As he died, we expressed our deepest love to him, and a flood of emotions overwhelmed us. We were moved and hopeful, but also terribly sad.

We three were there at the end holding his hand as he struggled to breath over that last hour. We prayed, read scripture, and reassured him we'd see him again in heaven one day. Of course, my mother's time and words with him are still clear to me today.

Among her most cherished moments was when she read a letter to him. The letter was not one either of them had written, but was rather written by a soldier to his wife during the Civil War, as he entered battle for the last time. My father had read that poem twenty years earlier at the funeral of one of his best friends. The line that resonated most with him (and really the only line I remember) was when the soldier reassures his wife that if he should die, she will see him "in the wind."

My father loved to sail, and we sailed together often in those last years. The wind was a perfect metaphor for his spirit that would live on after he was gone. At that moment, I took those words of my mother to heart. My father would certainly still live on in our hearts and in heaven, and we would remember him often, especially in the wind of a beautiful sailing day.

My father soon passed away, and we all silently mourned through our tears. As they prepared to take his deceased body away from us, my mother, brother, and I huddled in the next room. At that moment my phone pinged. Loudly, though, I thought it was silenced. I did not get many messages in those days, but a warning from the Weather Channel came across my phone and grabbed my attention.

It was an awkward moment until I looked down. There was a tornado warning in Charlotte. I was blown away (pun intended). I don't get messages from the Weather Channel, and we don't get tornados in Charlotte. But right after my father's passing, and just after reading his most meaningful and significant passage on death, a violent wind storm was headed our way. His spirit was alive and well.

Later that night, I was sleeplessly praying in bed. I was restless and looking for some peace myself, but also prayed that my father was at ease from his suffering. Meanwhile, that storm raged outside. Our windows shook, and the whole house seemed to move. I prayed a lot, but ultimately when I prayed for peace, I received another clear message.

All that noise around me—in the middle of the night, in the middle of that storm—stopped. It was sudden and startling. An immediate answer to my prayer. I went outside in our front yard and only a gentle breeze was left. I prayed more and thanked God for his salvation and his grace in reminding me of this fact in my most desperate hour.

From then on, the wind has been God's sign to me that my father is safe and secure in heaven.

I cannot then describe to you my complete shock to find my father, in the wind, in this song. At Nathan's most desperate hour, in the grips of a fatal depression, as he called out for some help from God, my father was there, ushering Nathan up his stairway to heaven.

Of course, now I realize that the wind is also one of the most common metaphors for the Holy Spirit. I feel completely sure that Nathan is now safe and secure in heaven, and that my father and the Holy Spirit were there to welcome him. Nathan, your stairway to heaven is with the wind. These words are forever etched in my heart, my mind, and my soul.

As the song concludes, its words are beautiful to me. It has given me a greater understanding of Nathan's depression and his wrestling with his place in this world. And it shows me how God led Nathan to him and to a place of peace and security.

In this world, sometimes our shadows overwhelm us, and our soul lives in fear. Nathan could not deal with his shadows for they loomed high and mighty. Depression is real, terrible, and dark—and for too many, fatal.

Thankfully, Nathan's story does not end there. Sarah and I consider these words sent to our hearts by God as the ultimate truth. Nathan now shines the white light of heaven, he points our hearts back to God, and hopefully we will all listen to his message and find our own way to this merciful salvation.

At first I wondered why Nathan was "buying" his way into heaven. This is not right, and of course none of us can "buy" our own way into heaven. It did not work for Nathan until he changed his mind, changed the path he was on at the last minute with a word of faith. Indeed, it is only through the grace and sacrifice of Jesus Christ that we are saved. So why this line to end the poem?

On the day of Nathan's funeral, a friend of mine texted me an image of a painting by Ron DiCianni (it is now printed and hangs in my office at home). In it, a person about Nathan's age seems worn out from their time on earth, approaches Jesus's throne, and falls to his knees with exhaustion. Jesus has come down off his throne, drops to his knees alongside this crushed soul, and embraces him. An angel looks over as Jesus comforts and consoles this broken soul, and welcomes him into heaven.

It is a beautiful depiction of a broken, earthly spirit welcomed into God's arms. After hanging it, though, I found out the title of it is "Safely Home (Jesus Welcomes the Martyr)." The person is meant by the artist to have sacrificed their life in the name of God. Having been persecuted for this, they are ultimately welcomed into God's arms for their work and sacrifice.

I still see Nathan's broken spirit welcomed into God's arms in that beautiful painting, even if he has not sacrificed as much as others here on this earth. I am sure Jesus still welcomes him as much as any other. To be sure, we are all his lost sheep.

For me, there is greater meaning in this title and in Nathan's buying his stairway to heaven. I hope that Nathan's death is a wake-up call for us all. Life is short. It is full of pain and suffering. And the only hope any of us really have in the end is the love of God and our salvation through Jesus Christ.

Thankfully, Nathan's death has turned my family closer to each other and to God, and so his death is not in vain. Hopefully, for others who have heard his story at the time or through this book, Nathan can be a martyr for you too. His death can be an opening for us all . . . an opportunity to recognize the evils of mental illness, to understand the desperate need for us to love each other more, and perhaps to begin to recognize that that love moves us all toward an everlasting communion.

Only if Nathan's death brings about some understanding of this in others will he be a martyr for some good in the world. It is up to you to allow God to use his death for positive change.

The song ends with a beautiful depiction of heaven. It is a place of equality, self-sacrifice, and without sin or evil. It is a wonderful place where we all live as one.

The original "rock" of the church was the disciple Peter. Jesus appointed him in this role, and did not change his mind or lose hope for Peter when he "rolled." Peter famously denied Jesus three times after Jesus was taken by the Roman soldiers, arrested, and crucified. Peter, the rock, rolled away from God.

Thank God that Jesus died for all our sins. Despite our faults, we are now invited to that perfect heaven, to be one with the Trinity, living together in perfect harmony, serving each other, and with no more fear of "rolling" away.

Jesus describes this unity best at The Last Supper. His last act at that supper when he was acutely aware of his imminent betrayal, judgement, and crucifixion was to pray for us.

In what is now known as the "High Priestly Prayer," Jesus speaks to his father on our behalf: "The glory which You have given Me I have given to them, that they may be one, just as We are one; I in them and You in Me, That they may be perfected in unity, so that the world may know that You sent Me, and loved them, even as You have loved Me. Father, I desire that they also, whom You have given Me, be with Me where I am, so that they may see My glory which You have given Me, for you loved Me before the foundation of the world" (John 17:22–24).

One day we all will be one with God, and I will be with my son, Nathan, again.

Question: What song reminds you of God? Or what artwork, poem, or story?

Action: Compile a collection of songs (or art or poems) that you can reference when in a particular mood. For example, create an album of songs that are uplifting for you when you're depressed, thought provoking if you're feeling introspective, exciting if you're getting ready to play sports, joyful if you're in love, or grateful if you're feeling blessed.

Epilogue 1

I nitially, I asked you to separate Nathan's character from his final act. Now I am going to ask you to separate Nathan's story from yours.

To be sure, there are important lessons to be learned from Nathan's story.

First, you are not alone. In fact, it is in leaning into those around you that there is hope. In Nathan's word's, "Do not overthink and just let the words come out. It has made this week so much easier."

Releasing the burdens of your depression is the first step toward getting better. Family, friends, and professionals are all vital to include in your own recovery.

Secondly, there is always a recovery. You will witness mine in the next part of this book, but there is a light in the future for you too.

If you are feeling down, inevitably, the only place to go is up. Have faith. Through perseverance, and with work, you will feel better.

Indeed, your story is not over.

American Suicide Prevention Lifeline (24/7): 800-273-8255

American Foundation for Suicide Prevention: www.afsp.org

Suicide Awareness/Voices of Education: www.save.org

Suicide Prevention Resource Center: www.sprc.org

Part II—**Me and You**

_ 9 _
Shock

T hey say the first stage of grief is shock. After Nathan died, Sarah and I were in shock for about a month, and it was truly a gift from God. We could not sleep; our thoughts were completely turned to the loss of Nathan. We prayed almost constantly and wandered aimlessly throughout our lives. Fortunately, there were meals from neighbors, letters poured in, relatives visited, and friends were constantly comforting us. They were everywhere before and after the funeral. We were cared for in every possible way.

Sarah and I both spoke at Nathan's funeral, a fact that surprised many people. How could we have emotionally gotten through such an act? Well, we were completely numb at that point. We were oblivious to our surroundings. In our shock, we were somehow shielded from the enormity of our loss. If God only gives us the amount of suffering that we can handle, then at that moment he was giving us very little understanding of what we were facing. That realization trickled in over the next months.

On the contrary, God was constantly sending us signs, reassuring us that he knew of Nathan's plight, was with him, and had him in his arms. We were laser focused on this message. It was the foundation upon which we stood. I would tell anyone who wanted to know that it was not a matter of faith at that point, but knowledge in God's salvation.

Today, I can more clearly look back and see that for all the good we received from friends and family—for all the assurances of Nathan's salvation—it did not add up to nearly enough to compensate for the loss of our son. Somehow we were calmer and more comforted than we should have been. At the time, I said to Sarah, "Why are we so calm and at peace?"

My only explanation is that the enormity of our loss was taken away by the shock we were experiencing. It was a blessing, sheltering us from our grief and surrounding us with comfort in our darkest hour. Even now, years later, we can only contemplate our loss in little bits at a time before we fall into a deep grief. God comes to us most obviously in our hour of need, and at that time Sarah and I were closer to him than ever before.

In the famous poem "Footprints," the writer looks back on his life as he walks along the beach. Along the way, he notices two sets of footprints as God is walking with him. However, the author comes to the realization that in the worst moments of his life, there was only one set of footprints in the sand.

"How can this be?" he asks God. "Did you abandon me in my greatest time of need?" God's reply is simple but profound. "It was in those times of need, that I was carrying you." The one set was not the author's but rather God's.

Immediately after Nathan's death, Sarah and I felt comforted and insulated, free from the agony of what our life had become. We were being carried through this tragedy by God.

A Bible verse was brought to my attention more than once at this time. It was Psalm 34:18: "The Lord is near to the broken-hearted and saves those who are crushed in spirit."

Part of the comfort in this simple verse was that Nathan himself was clearly crushed in spirit. God had not saved him in the way we would have wished. Indeed, I prayed to God after his first cry for help—when he ran away six months before his death—that I could somehow reach him, comfort him, and help him overcome his demons. I would have given anything to struggle alongside Nathan with his depression, working to overcome it.

But when Nathan seemed lost a second time, I began to pray even harder. This time, though, I began to pray that God would take over where I was inadequate, touching Nathan's heart and mind, and turning him to a comforting faith. But the world is a difficult place, full of the evils of depression and death. Ultimately, God saved Nathan in his own way, not on this earth.

We, of course, were brokenhearted. In those days that Nathan was missing—and in the weeks after his passing—we prayed a lot. We spoke to friends, opened up our hearts, and shared our sorrow. We questioned the meaning of it all. We were lost, so we often asked God for clarity. And he delivered, time and again.

Even in the moment, it seemed every time I asked for answers, God answered directly and immediately. We felt his presence. He was near to us.

I often pray over that painting "Safely Home," which hangs in my office. It is a beautiful reminder of where Nathan is today. For sure, especially in those initial weeks and months, I could only remember Nathan in heaven, at peace and safe with God. Any reminders of his depression and death brought agony. Thoughts of better times in his youth were just reminders of how much of a promising life was now lost.

I can never experience the joy of life with Nathan again. But I can look forward to that glorious, heavenly embrace God prepares for all of us beyond our time here on earth.

Now when I look to that picture, I see myself as much as Nathan. Often I'm so weakened by grief that I feel myself crumble into the arms of God. And he always seems to catch me. In fact, I welcome that embrace as the only place where I can find true refuge. For my soul is broken too.

I now view the physical "shock" we suffered after Nathan's death as a spiritual experience. More specifically, I believe it was the Holy Spirit—the most misunderstood person of the Trinity—who was with us throughout this time. Indeed, I still feel his presence today.

Let me elaborate on the most important means of my recovery—my relationship with God, and my understanding of his love for us all—as made possible through the Holy Spirit.

Question: C. S. Lewis (*Mere Christianity*) stated: "There is one vice of which no man in the world is free . . . . There is no fault which makes a man more unpopular, and no fault which we are more unconscious of in ourselves . . . . The vice I am talking of is pride or self-conceit: and the virtue opposite to it, in Christian morals, is called humility." What experiences in life have left you feeling humbled or out of control? Did this ultimately help you become more grounded and/or closer to God?

Action: Be subservient to someone you live with for a week. What lessons did you learn? How did it make you feel? What rewards did you receive?

10

The Holy Comforter

I n the book of John, Jesus first brings up the Holy Spirit in chapter 7. In the middle of Jesus' ministry, he is in Jerusalem on the last day of the Festival of Tabernacles. The people are once again questioning Jesus' works and his importance in their faith. The Pharisees are threatening to arrest him. Jesus responds with a metaphor: "If anyone is thirsty, let him come to Me and drink. He who believes in Me, as the Scripture said, 'From his innermost being will flow rivers of living water'" (John 7:37–38).

John then clarifies what Jesus is speaking about, "But this He spoke of the Spirit, whom those who believed in Him were to receive; for the Spirit was not yet given, because Jesus was not yet glorified" (John 7:39).

John often quoted Jesus' use of bread and water as symbols of the way to the kingdom of heaven. In John 6:50-51, Jesus is the "living bread," which enables one to "live forever." In John 4:14, Jesus tells the woman at the well that "whoever drinks of the water that I will give him shall never thirst."

In these passages, Jesus is addressing those who hunger and thirst for him—those who believe and seek out the truth of God in Jesus. The bread and water he offers fully quenches this desire, and we become completely satisfied in God.

To me this passage speaks of the Holy Spirit as our comforter. The one who comes to us (as a gift) and satisfies all our earthly needs and desires. He embraces us with the knowledge of God's love for us, our salvation through Jesus Christ, and the hope of eternal life.

At the Last Supper, Jesus again speaks of the Holy Spirit. "If you love Me, you will keep My commandments. I will ask the Father, and He will give you another Helper, that He may be with you forever" (John 14:15–16). And, "I tell you the truth, it is to your advantage that I go away; for if I do not go away, the Helper [Spirit] will not come to you; but if I go, I will send Him to you" (John 16:7).

The word used to describe the Holy Spirit in the book of John is the Greek word *parakletos* (or in English today, paraclete). The word literally means "to call (*kalein*) to one's side (*para*)." It is often used to describe an advocate that people would call in court to defend their cases. John uses the word in this specific way when he described Jesus in his first letter: 1 John, chapter 2 ("And if anyone sins, we have an Advocate with the Father, Jesus Christ the righteous.").

In the Gospel of John, the term is perhaps better interpreted as a comforter or helper. Indeed, Jesus refers to the Holy Spirit as one he is sending to comfort us in times of suffering, and to help us not just in times of trouble, but also to generally guide us in the truth.

Interestingly, with the Greek word John uses in his Gospel, he places the accent over the second "a" in *parakletos*. This is important since when the accent is placed here (as opposed to over the "o" at the end of the word), the actions of this "helper" are ever-present. The Holy Spirit is being described as a permanent comforter working alongside us to instill the peace of God in our souls.

The Holy Spirit revealed himself to me in the form of my shock after Nathan's death. I believe it was the Holy Spirit who gave Sarah and me this initial period of numbness. He comforted us more than we could imagine. As great as our grief, the love and security from the Holy Spirit was greater.

Sarah will tell you it was the Holy Spirit who put the image in her mind of Nathan in his green Led Zeppelin shirt the last time she saw him. It was the Spirit who directed us to the song

"Stairway to Heaven," giving us some peace and understanding from Nathan's point of view.

When Nathan was lost during those first four days, Sarah made a habit of spending the night sitting by a front window in our house. The window looked out onto our driveway and in her sleeplessness, she waited for the first sign that Nathan was returning home. Outside the window is a large tree, and that tree seemed to embrace the scene and offer her comfort. In the bark, she saw a face and felt as if God was looking down on her, offering peace, and protection. The Holy Spirit embraced her in his love.

Nathan of course did not return home, and now that we know his fate, that face feels like it was Nathan's to her. He now looks down from heaven, offering her the peace and comfort that he now experiences in heaven. This image is still a gift from the Spirit to her.

We notice now that tree has two low branches that reach out and frame Sarah's window. The branches look eerily similar to the arms of the Led Zeppelin fallen angel. This angel is Nathan. In agony on this earth, but now heavenly saved and at peace.

I vividly remember one night about two weeks after Nathan's death. I lay in bed caught up in doubt and uncertainty. As much as God had been there speaking to me and reassuring me of Nathan's safety, I had not experienced this from Nathan himself. I prayed to Nathan directly. I was devastated by his suffering and asked him if he was alright, if he was indeed happy and safe. After a few hours alone like this in bed, I finally nodded off.

Immediately, Nathan came to me in a dream. He was the center of attention, laughing and joking as a small boy, entertaining the whole family in our kitchen. He suddenly stopped, grew into the young man he had become, and approached me. Everything quieted as he leaned over and whispered in my ear, "It's alright dad. You don't have to worry anymore. I'm fine."

Tears filled my eyes as I woke, startled by the reality of my vision, and at peace again in Nathan's salvation. This dream had answered my prayers. The Holy Spirit had reached out to me again and offered hopeful answers.

Of course, shock is only the first stage of grief. As I struggled with the subsequent phases of my life after the death of my son, those other stages consumed me as well. But the Spirit never left. He walks with us through any and all valleys. And he makes himself known to us still today as intimately as possible.

Question: Dr. Martin Luther King Jr. said, "The ultimate measure of a man is not where he stands in moments of comfort and convenience, but where he stands at times of challenge and controversy." What is it that makes your heart uneasy? Where does God stir your soul?

Action: Dr. Martin Luther King Jr. also said, "Those who are not looking for happiness are the most likely to find it, because those who are searching forget that the surest way to be happy is to seek happiness for others." Donate time or resources to a charity. Pick something meaningful to you and be a blessing to someone else.

11

The Downward Turn

A s I've moved on from my shock, more familiar emotions of grief emerged. There are many models of the stages of grief, but one seven-stage list seems particularly appropriate to me. In this explanation, the seven stages of grief include: shock and denial; pain and guilt; anger; bargaining; depression; the upward turn; reconstruction and working through; and acceptance and hope.

I don't necessarily think of these emotions as stages one works through. Rather, I'm consigned to the fact that all the "stages" of grief are now a permanent part of my life. I'm getting used to the new reality of living without my son; and as such, all these emotions seem to come daily.

People say when you go through such a tragedy as this, you need to get used to a new life. Things will always be different going forward. For me, that means getting used to living in the dark. My goal in life is no longer joy or happiness. Grief is a constant companion, and that is okay.

Pain and guilt are heart-wrenching parts of grieving for a parent who's lost a child, and that is certainly true when your child commits suicide. Sympathy for us generates from the terrible fact that no one deserves to live through such a thing. No matter how inefficient our parenting styles were, mental illness is now a tragic reality we will never escape.

Our love is genuine, and our loss is profound. Death is part of life, but it can be so cruel. So many people have told us, "There is nothing you could have done," or "He's in a better place now," or "God works in mysterious ways."

I suppose that offers some comfort—in a cumulative manner. Nathan is gone, though, and we were part of that then, and still suffer the consequences now.

Years later, it is still difficult for Sarah and me to talk about Nathan. There are moments when we can remember the joy he brought to our lives. This, no question, makes it all worth it. Our love for him cannot be replaced, and we would go through this all over again for the special light he gave us.

Our deep love for him is reflected by the heartache in losing him. And that more often is what we are left with. Inevitably, any conversations with Sarah turn to that loss, and we break down in the anguish.

Mostly, Sarah and I experience the stages of grief at different times from one another. Everyone must grieve in their own way. I have become more deliberate in my recovery, reaching out to others and never missing a moment to discuss my pain and loss. Sarah is more patient. She is also more hesitant to face the pain of her loss. She would prefer to be distracted by more pleasant pursuits and busy herself with work and other activities.

We both live life largely to survive, going our own separate paths and supporting each other only briefly when those paths happen to intertwine. Our marital relationship has taken a back seat to our personal recovery. Love still binds us, but grief gets in the way and has created a terrible valley between us. We often suffer separately, alone. And that just adds to the sense of loss.

I also have had significant moments of denial and bargaining. Nathan's body was found, identified, cremated, and buried. However, sometimes I cling to the hope that in God all things are possible. I've often prayed and reassured God that if he chooses to allow Nathan to walk through our front door and return to our life restored, that I will have no problem believing in that miracle. I can imagine it happening and would happily accept it as a perfectly fine reality.

Why can't the thin spaces between heaven and earth dissolve for just long enough to let Nathan return to me? If it did, I would be sure to glorify God and let the world know the miracles he can perform.

I have also cursed out Nathan many times when obsessing about his death. Sometimes it relieves tension. "Nathan, you stupid a-hole!" "Why didn't you just f'ing talk to someone." "How could you be so dumb as to turn a temporary situation into a permanent tragedy." "Why didn't you understand what this would do to us!"

I also get mad at God. Sometimes I echo Mary and Martha after their brother, Lazarus, died. "Lord, if only you were here, Nathan wouldn't have died." God's answers to my prayers are never completely satisfactory.

Most of my anger now is directed at the devil. Before Nathan died, as a scientist and physician, I enjoyed reading the Bible literally. I could understand the science of the creation, the star of Bethlehem, the parting of the Red Sea, and the burning bush. Many of the miracles of the Old and New Testament can be understood scientifically.

I often thought of the ills that Jesus cured in such a way. For example, in Mark 5, a man named Legion was consumed by convulsions. To me, it is clear he had intractable epilepsy, seizing day and night.

The Bible, however, describes Legion as "of unclean spirit" and "possessed by the devil." I had always thought of this description as more symbolic. But perhaps God's description of Legion's plight is more accurate. From God's point of view (in his word), Legion was a victim of the devil, of evil on this earth. When Jesus rids him of these demons, Legion is cured of his physical disease.

I actually prefer this description of disease now. Many evils—through sin—we bring on ourselves. Adultery, murder, and hate come immediately to mind. But there are also evils of this world that are not directly merited. Natural disasters, disease, mental illness, and death do not discriminate. I believe when David tells us he "fears no evil" or when Jesus asks us to pray in The Lord's Prayer "deliver us from evil," these are some of those evils.

Nathan, I am sure would agree, was consumed by demons. I now view his struggles as an evil that took over his mind, that he was unprepared to conquer, and which ultimately destroyed him. That is where I channel my anger these days. I personify the evil that led to the circumstance of Nathan's death, and I hate it.

I blame Satan.

I abhor the imperfections of this world that led to Nathan's depression. I detest the incongruities of our personalities that prevented us from effectively helping him. And I loathe the overwhelming impulses that forced Nathan to believe there was no hope for the future.

David Bentley Hart once wrote specifically about a deadly tsunami and about death in general: "Our faith is in a God who has come to rescue His creation from the absurdity of sin and the emptiness of death, and so we are permitted to hate these things with a perfect hatred . . . . When I see the death of a child, I do not see the face of God, but the face of His enemy."

I take solace in the fact that one day God "will wipe away every tear from their eyes; and there will no longer be any death" (Rev 21:4). Nathan is now delivered into heaven, and someday God will deliver us from all these evils as well. The devil will be no more.

More than lashing out at Nathan or Jesus, I find myself these days screaming, "F— you, Satan! You cannot bring me or Nathan down!"

At the lowest levels of our grief, Sarah and I muddle through life: alone and angry, downtrodden and afraid. This is the most defining aspect of grief. Thankfully, though, as time passes, the stages of grief also involve an upward turn. That upward turn first manifested itself to me in the form of a poem.

Question: When have you been depressed in your life? How long did it last? Who or what helped you work your way out of it?

Action: Read a book on depression or loss. The ones that helped me in my initial shock and loss were: *Darkness Visible* by William Styron, *When Bad Things Happen to Good People* by Harold Kushner, *Life After the Death of My Son* by Dennis Apple, and *Walking with God Through Pain and Suffering* by Timothy Keller.

12

Prophetic Words

After Nathan died, I still attended Bible study with my friends even though my purpose there and my perspective had changed. I attribute my recovery from Nathan's death to the work of the Holy Spirit. My spiritual community with my faithful friends is a large part of that, and I'm grateful for them to be part of my healing process.

God's love is often manifested in others. Hopefully, I give back to them as well. I can demonstrate that no matter how difficult life seems—no matter how terrible our circumstances here on earth—God ultimately has a plan for us all.

Shortly after Nathan's death, I was asked to lead a Bible study. Our group had been following an online study of the Bible, but I had not yet recovered enough to read and meditate on the Word. I had no idea what book of the Bible we were on or what we had been studying. I normally just showed up on Friday mornings and leant my perspective.

But as the leader, I had to prepare something. I opened www.hereadstruth.com on my phone and read the day's lesson. Once again, it felt like God had reached down to me personally and sent a message of his love and compassion. That week's lesson happened to be Psalm 23:

> The Lord is my shepherd,
>
> I shall not want.
>
> He makes me lie down in green pastures;

He leads me beside quiet waters.

He restores my soul;

He guides me in the paths of righteousness

For His name's sake.

Even though I walk through the valley of the shadow of death,

I fear no evil, for You are with me;

Your rod and Your staff, they comfort me.

You prepare a table before me in the presence of my enemies;

You have anointed my head with oil;

My cup overflows.

Surely goodness and lovingkindness shall follow me
all the days of my life,

And I will dwell in the house of the Lord forever.

This psalm has been memorized by many faithful Christians and is often used at funeral services. It is relevant for all of us as it beautifully describes God's relationship with us. It gives me great comfort and is now one of my most cherished prayers. Its words are incredible and important to me now, and I truly consider them a gift from God. It brings perspective to my life with Nathan and encompasses my entire journey of faith.

Its author is David, one of the most significant figures of the Old Testament. He was a lowly shepherd who grew up to be a great king of Israel. The youngest of eight sons, David got the worst jobs. In those days, that meant being a shepherd—devoting countless days and nights alone in the fields caring for his family's sheep

While it was difficult, David knew the job of a shepherd was vitally important. He provided everything for his sheep and acted as their guide, provider, healer, comforter, protector, governor, and lifeline. What's more, a shepherd leads his flock. He is not a cowboy wrangling his herd, scaring the cattle into a group from behind, engaging in fear and chaos to move them in the direction he wants. The shepherd leads his flock from the front. He walks ahead of them, guiding them out of danger and toward food and shelter and safety. And the sheep follow.

In the first half of this psalm, David lays out the foundations of his faith. He begins with, "The Lord is my Shepherd." In one simple sentence he is confessing that the Lord is his guide and provider in all things. He is recognizing that God leads the way in our path of salvation. Jesus uses this metaphor of the shepherd and his sheep twice in his teachings. Perhaps he was thinking of this psalm when he gave these two messages.

First is the parable of the lost sheep found in Luke 15. In it, the shepherd values the life of every single sheep in his flock. He will leave all in order go after "that which is lost." Upon finding that sheep, he rejoices. God values each of us with equal fervor, and rejoices when we hear his word and follow him.

Jesus further explains the meaning of this relationship in John 10:14-15: "I am the good Shepard, and I know My own and My own know Me . . . and I lay down My life for the sheep." Jesus not only provides a tangible image of who God is but also willingly gave up his own life to save us all.

David also surely realizes that in this metaphor he is the sheep. We all need to humble ourselves before God and surrender ourselves to his authority. A sheep is a frightful animal, prone to wandering. If left alone, sheep are rarely calm. They will not trust any other sheep in their own flock. They will not eat, drink, rest, or survive.

We are similar: lost, needy, and prone to straying from our Lord. Only when we listen to his voice—attentively and constantly submit to his guidance—are we able to live life freely, safe, and secure.

David realizes with the Lord on his (and our) side that "I shall not want."

Jesus again explains this idea better than I could. Luke 12:22-31 says: "For this reason I say to you, do not worry about your life, as to what you will eat; nor for your body, as to what you will put on . . . Consider the ravens, for they neither sow nor reap; they have no storeroom nor barn, and yet God feeds them . . .

Consider the lilies, how they grow: they neither toil nor spin; but I tell you, not even Solomon in all his glory clothed himself like one of these . . . And do not seek what yo₁   ₁at and what you will drink, and do not keep worrying .   ᵗˢ kingdom, and these things will be added to you'

What beautiful, reassuring wor₁ fore they were even uttered.

"I shall not want" is not just presented as ₁ be interpreted as a command. We all worship someₙ₁ material things, people, ideas, or the Lord. This verse, as muₐ₁ anything, is a call to refocus our desires on the one necessary thing in our lives: the Lord.

Paul echoes David in his letter to the Romans, "For the mind set on the flesh is death, but the mind set on the Spirit is life and peace" (Rom 8:6).

If Nathan's death has taught me anything, it is that this world is flawed. Nothing in our life will endure forever, and our desires are a fragile foundation upon which to rest our hopes and expectations.

I know when Nathan was struggling I prayed that God would help him. When he went missing, I asked God to return him safely. I desperately wanted a miracle for Nathan and us. Even today, I yearn to see him again and curse the circumstances and evils that consumed him. I often wish I could dictate the fate of this world to establish my personal comfort and security.

But that is not the way of our world. "To set the mind on the flesh is death." Nathan's salvation has only come in spirit. His life comes from beyond this world to that of the Lord. The Spirit is everything good that life gives. We should not want for anything more.

In the next line, the sheep is made to "lie down" in green pastures. W. Phillip Keller in his book, *A Shepherd Looks at Psalm 23*, points out the criteria that must be met in order for a sheep to actually calm down enough to lie down. First, the sheep must be well fed. Second, they must feel secure. Third, they must feel no friction among the other sheep. And finally, they must feel healthy.

This is no easy task for such a foolish animal. Yet the shepherd provides all this to them. Not only does the Lord provide food and water for us in the "green pastures" and "still waters," but he also provides safety, security, and health.

If we have surrendered ourselves to the Lord, then he leads us. And he "leads us beside still waters." This verse references not just the water we need to survive, but also the peace we all seek in God's welcoming arms. Once we are secure in our faith, nothing can touch us. There is a peace in our soul that is life giving.

John the Baptist's father references this verse in his prophesying in Luke 1:79, stating Jesus has come, "To shine upon those who sit in darkness and the shadow of death, To guide our feet into the way of peace."

Remember how Jesus uses water as a symbol of the life he gives to each of us? Remember what he told the Samaritan woman at a well in John chapter 4? "Whoever drinks of the water that I will give him shall never thirst; but the water that I will give him will become in him a well of water springing up to eternal life."

In the next verse, the Lord "restores my soul." He provides our salvation. In faith, humbly recognizing all that the Lord provides—in surrendering to his love and grace, and in following his lead—we are saved.

Restore is defined as "to bring return to a former condition" or "to repair or renovate." In our salvation—possible by the sacrifice of Jesus—we are restored to our perfect condition that was ours upon creation before the original sin. Just as important, we are restored to that community with God we can enjoy with a renewed soul.

These first passages speak of David's faith. They directly point to the Lord, but also to Jesus Christ and to the Holy Spirit. God always loved us, and shows this throughout the Old Testament in promising and working toward a renewal of our relationship with him. That message is clear in David's prayer.

In the New Testament, we see that promise first physically fulfilled in the form of Jesus Christ, and then permanently through the Holy Spirit. Jesus leads the way though. He came down to earth and first showed us who the Lord is and how to live with him. He then perfectly sacrificed himself for us that we may also experience this wonderful relationship. He has restored our soul, and this realization is the culmination of our becoming a Christian.

As believers, our focus is rightly on Jesus. And in having faith in him and following his example, we are compelled to good works. Paul, in his letter to the Ephesians, explains the nature of our salvation: "For by grace you have been saved through faith; and that not of yourselves, it is the gift of God; not as a result of works" (Eph 2:8).

But Paul does not stop there. He then says, "For we are His workmanship, created in Christ Jesus for good works" (Eph 2:8–10). Once we are saved through our faith in Jesus, we are transformed; we are created to do "good works."

We are meant to walk down the "paths of righteousness." But not for our own salvation. That has already been secured and is not our own doing. We are to do good works for "his name's sake" in order to glorify God. We are called to do these acts of righteousness by our faith and the realization of all that God has given us. And then compelled to do them in thanks and praise of the grace God has shown us.

To me, our spiritual transformation should mirror David's. He spells out what it takes to initiate a lasting relationship with God. David's journey is the same we all must take to experience the living God within us. We're all on different points of our spiritual journey and we all fall short in many ways, but God is always there for us, guiding and comforting us along the way.

This does not fully explain our path though. The psalm takes a dramatic, personal turn at this point. Gone are the niceties of our generalized, comfortable religion. David now brings us into the dirt of our imperfect lives. We find ourselves with him, deep down in the valley of struggle, pain, suffering, and death. Still, we are not alone.

Here the psalm stops referring to God in the impersonal third person. As we step into the frightening unknown of this world, it is critical to realize that God is intimately with us. A revelation that is so important that David now begins to address God directly. "You are with me."

Question: Where are you on your spiritual journey? Where do you want to be?

Action: Practice the Prayer of Examen at the end of each day for a week. https://www.ignatianspirituality.com/ignatian-prayer/the-examen/how-can-i-pray/

13

The Valley of the Shadow of Death

O nce we understand and begin our life in Christ, the fruits of this relationship are many. Enduring the tragedies of this world without this understanding is to be without hope—and seems impossible to me. Sometimes this world's circumstances can overwhelm us, which is where I found myself after Nathan's death.

You, too, have likely suffered from personal trials and struggles. We all must move through our own valleys. Thankfully, we are not alone. Jesus Christ leads the way into and through this valley, and the Holy Spirit remains there with us today.

As David journeys through the valley of the shadow of death in this psalm, his language changes from speaking about God to speaking directly to him. "Even though I walk through the valley of the shadow of death, I fear no evil, for You are with me."

David's words are beautiful and so perfect for all of us who struggle. As did David, we need to remind ourselves of God's presence.

After Nathan died, I was certainly lost in a deep valley of despair, surrounded by shadows, dark thoughts, and deep uncertainty. Only with the comfort of God do I find the strength to survive. Keep in mind, these evils we experience on earth are but a shadow, an illusion, an immaterial mirage.

Jesus walked through this valley and conquered death so we no longer need to fear. He's been through all the temptations and tribulations we experience and understands our struggles. He has been persecuted, ostracized, and tortured worse than any of us could imagine. He left heaven to suffer for our sake. Jesus has made even death to be but a fleeting shadow, a dark apparition that can no longer harm us.

I am aware now more than ever that death is part of life. We all will be touched by death many times. At the very least, we will have to come to grips with our own death. Of course, having a child die—and die by suicide—brings its own emotions that make one's recovery especially challenging.

Feelings of what might have been for Nathan as well as my own guilt and shame compound my deep sorrow. I have been through every circumstance and scenario of his death many times over. I relive the pain of his death daily. I blame everything and everyone. And I am tempted to be frustrated, angry, and hopeless at the injustice of it all. Especially since it happened for seemingly unnecessary causes or maybe could have been avoided somehow.

At times, I'm paralyzed and just plain depressed by this overwhelming tragedy. For my own depression, I am medicated now with the same SSRI that would have been so appropriate for Nathan. It helps. I am also determined not to repeat Nathan's mistakes in dealing with his depression.

I have resolved not to suffer through this alone. Only God's love can conquer evil, especially death. For me, that love is manifest in the form of God's creation: other people.

One of the first things I did after Nathan died was to sign up for a Facebook account in an effort to connect better with friends and family. I have joined more Bible studies and support groups and am not afraid to open up about my circumstances. I am now the dad whose son killed himself, and I need to own that. Pouring out my soul and becoming vulnerable is somewhat cathartic to me now. The love and compassion I receive in return helps chip away at my sorrow.

Whatever consequences come my way from opening up are immaterial and minuscule compared to what I've already been through. In fact, I have not experienced negative effects of communicating with others, and received only love and compassion in return.

Shortly after Nathan died, his rugby club adopted the slogan "Never Walk Alone." It speaks to my heart now more than they know.

Taber had just started college during this terrible time. He was going back to Auburn where they take pride in being one big Auburn "family." Being surrounded by others, especially as a loving family, often seems like the only way to counter the anguish death brings.

Jesus knows how difficult our time on earth can be. God, our Father, understands my grief, for he too has lost his son. How hard must it have been for him to send Jesus from heaven, down into this valley. It must have been something like what I'll experience for the next thirty years or so. Life without my son by my side can be lonely and sad. It is only the great miracle of salvation that makes it bearable. In my misery, this is comforting indeed.

For Sarah, this reminder of God leading the way for us even in death came when we took a family trip to Rome. We were moved by Michelangelo's "Pieta" sculpture, in which the Virgin Mary cradles the body of her just crucified son. It is the painful conclusion of the passion of Christ, before any of Jesus' followers understood the miraculous implications to come. Not only did Jesus and our Father feel the pain of this sacrifice, but so did those around him, especially his mother.

Thankfully, we can now rejoice in the glory of this sacrifice. Jesus led the way for us in death, but he also conquered death and guides us into the kingdom of heaven.

This valley now has a way out; this shadow has a shining light behind it, waiting to welcome us into its fold. It sometimes seems we are overwhelmed by not only the evils of sin, cruelty, and hate, but of disease, cancer, mental illness, and death. One way or another, we are all affected, but we need not fear. God knows the way beyond these afflictions, and he is willing to show us.

Just as David, we no longer need to feel alone in these struggles. Our faith is rewarded with a deep, personal relationship with God. "You are with me," says David.

In David's time, this was a bold statement. God was elusive and only really seemed to show himself to a select few. For us today, this statement is even more relevant. As I have experienced firsthand, God is ever-present within us. When Jesus secured our salvation and was seated on the right hand of God our Father, he left us with an amazing gift—the Holy Spirit—who resides in our hearts and souls. He, the Spirit, is with us now and forever.

Jesus conquered death. Before that he had to die. And during his life he suffered. At Lazarus' tomb, Jesus cried at the sadness of his death right before he was to raise him from the dead. God's love is constant. He responds to all our sadness with the same tears. He also responds with a vigorous love that can overcome whatever we are going through.

When we learn to let go of this life and give it over to God, we begin to see that his steady hand is all we can rest in—and that is good. I'm confident Nathan is resting there now, and our time is yet to come.

God's means to help us through our trials are as infinite as his love. But David describes it from the perspective of a shepherd. The Spirit, like a shepherd, now wields the "rod" and "staff." The shepherd's rod is a weapon and a means to protect and discipline his sheep. It is a symbol of God's power and authority over us, and in the Old Testament most often brought about fear. But David welcomes and finds comfort in the overwhelming might of our God. And we should too.

Jesus' example of how to live, his overcoming the temptations of this earth, and his reminders to us today of the ways to live in righteousness should bring us peace and comfort. The Gospels teach us the value and security that come with leading a God-centered life. Only in recognizing the glory God provides—and in working through him—can we experience the joy, peace, and freedoms that he intends for us.

Just as God's rod reminds us of our need to continue in the paths of righteousness, a shepherd's staff helps guide lost sheep back to the flock, keeps them stronger as a group, and shows them the way to food, water, and shelter. God provides us with all we need. He is our protector and our shield.

The story of Noah reminds me of this role of God. After bringing down a horrendous flood on the earth and enacting his discipline on his people with devastating consequences, God places a rainbow in the sky to promise us he will never again bring such judgement on us.

The Hebrew word for "rainbow," however, is not what we think. The word is actually translated as a "bow," as in a bow and arrow. After using his bow—his rod—to such effect, God hangs it in the sky, promising never to allow such an overwhelming disaster again. As this bow now hangs in the sky, it no longer points down at us, but is directed up at God himself.

There is still pain and suffering in our world, but God has promised to take it upon himself. He is reminding us that Jesus has come to sacrifice himself for all the consequences of our sin. He reigns in that authoritative judgement and extends a guiding hand to show us the way into a beautiful, safe, secure relationship with him. As such, we should all find comfort in God's rod and staff, especially at those times when we need them so much.

As frightful as our time on earth can be—as many demons and evils surround us—our Holy Father understands our pain. Jesus has been here to save us from it. And the Holy Spirit is here to guide us back to these truths. They are with us and eager to welcome us into their open arms.

In ancient times, welcoming someone into your home was a significant gesture. It was akin to giving one's word to provide food, shelter, and protection. Jesus, as he traveled in his day, was often welcomed into others' homes and offered dinner and companionship. Everyone fully understood the significance of this gesture. They were welcoming Jesus into their lives, and he was more than eager to enter theirs.

Similarly, Jesus' last supper shared with his disciples was a critical gesture. At its most basic level, Jesus was symbolically promising his disciples to provide for them. He was physically demonstrating the binding contract he was about to provide for them with his death.

They did not understand the full implications of this promise at the time, but Jesus was demonstrating through this meal—this supper—God's covenant to take on that punishment for our sin. Through his perfect sacrifice that defeated death and allowed us to engage with a permanent communion with him for all eternity.

Just as Jesus did on that last day of his life, God still today "prepares a banquet before us in the presence of our enemies." David beautifully spells this out for us!

Psalm 23 continues, "You anoint my head with oil." From a shepherd's point of view, this is yet another way he cares for his sheep. To anoint the sheep's head with oil, the shepherd is providing protection from the annoying flies and a healing salve to sooth any sores or infections on their face.

It reminds me of the Last Supper when Jesus knelt before his disciples to wash their feet. And in Peter's case, Jesus had no problem washing his feet and head as well, drying them with his robe. "In order to be first, you must be last." "I am the good shepherd and I lay down my life for the sheep." Indeed, in relation to all that God has given us, "Our cup runs over!" How could David or we interpret our relationship with God any other way?

Next, "Surely goodness and mercy shall follow me all the days of my life." God is good. And the promise of heaven is beyond imagination. The glory and greatness of our future with God are incredible. The heights to which our relationship with God will take us is astronomical. No amount of suffering or despair can take that away.

It is thrilling to imagine how glorious and amazing that future with our Lord will be, particularly when times on earth are so devastating. Remember as far up as we have to go to heaven is how far down Jesus came to reach us. I love to imagine Nathan in the peace and bliss of heaven, his pain and turmoil on earth now a distant memory.

Yet, it is our human nature to feel sorry for ourselves. It is so easy to lose perspective. To remember Nathan's last months is still devastating to me. I feel a great depression in realizing how much he must have suffered, and in knowing my own inadequacies in helping him. He was left lonely and horribly sad.

And I am left remorseful, depressed, and empty. It is this pain and suffering that also remind us of our need for God's grace and salvation. God still provides. The Spirit still gives abundantly. And our cup still runs over, even on this earth.

Our charge is to recognize that gift and mirror that heavenly relationship with others, and to glorify God in the process. We are sinful. We have brought this evil upon ourselves: directly and indirectly. Yet we are still the recipients of infinite glory, mercy, and hope.

We are blessed to be reminded of this by David: to hear the word of the Lord, recognize the works of Jesus for us and the Spirit within us, and understand all that has been given us. "Surely, goodness and lovingkindness shall follow us all the days of our life!"

Hope is a powerful emotion. Without it, Nathan was reduced to ashes. For all of us, nothing on this earth ultimately means much without God's promise for our future. It is everything. And it is absolutely ours. David's last line expresses this hope, not as a wish or idea, but as an absolute certainty: "I will dwell in the house of the Lord forever."

Sometimes others compliment Sarah and me for how we have dealt with Nathan's death. They say, "Your faith is so strong," and "How do you do it?" We have been blessed with so many signs from the Spirit of God that I feel certain of Nathan's salvation. I'm convinced of God's love, mercy, and gifts.

I no longer refer to it as my "faith" that sustains me, but my "knowledge" that he is with me, and he is guiding and protecting me. He is my Healer, my Comforter, my Guide, my Provider, and my Savior. This is my hope for you, too, that you will come to "know" that the Lord is your Shepherd and, ultimately, dwell in the house of the Lord forever.

The "stages" of grief are not at all like a stairway one needs to climb to reach some higher level of inner peace. Rather, each stage is a constantly present, powerful emotion that stays with you the rest of your life.

Interestingly, though, part of that complete experience of grief, by definition, includes some positive effects. These are the latter stages of grief that initially seem impossibly optimistic. They are the upward turn; reconstruction and working through; and acceptance and hope. Eventually, by the grace of God, these stages start to miraculously find their way into your heart.

> **Question:** What characteristic of sheep do you relate to? Insecurity; lacking trust in others; anxious about your job, personal life, or health; or prone to straying from your God? Does knowing God is by your side at all times help with your troubles?

> **Action:** Take care of yourself professionally (attend therapy), personally (attend a Bible study, book or social club, or play a sport), or individually (schedule an activity your family can do each week: game night, walk the neighborhood, go out to eat).

14

A New Hope

Restructuring one's life, working through the pain, and moving forward with hope are vital parts of the grieving process. They are part of my new life now too. I've definitely agonized through each step of this way as emotionally as anyone could endure. It has not been enjoyable.

It is equally sad to look ahead to a life without Nathan. But I have begun to grow and recover. The pain and depression do not disappear, but hope and faith are becoming more dominant aspects of my new life without Nathan.

For all the pain and darkness that Nathan suffered and that surrounds our family now, at least we know for sure that Nathan is safe, secure, and joyful in God's loving embrace. He is free of the burdens that destroyed him on earth. And we have a lot to look forward to in community with him and the Trinity when our time on earth is done. For that I am eternally grateful.

I certainly would not have wanted to go through this without that knowledge. In many ways, our human stubbornness only allows us to grow toward God through significant trials and struggles. Our pride is such that we need to be humbled frequently to recognize our dependence on God for everything.

I certainly did not grasp the magnitude of his grace prior to Nathan's tragic death. Now I realize that there is nothing worthwhile on this earth without the Lord's love for us, and Jesus' sacrifice. I thought I understood this before. I worked toward growing closer to God through church, Bible study, prayer, and communion with friends. But I was merely understanding God's love intellectually and not experiencing it emotionally or spiritually.

Now my faith has exceeded any knowledge of God's truth, and has developed into a deep desire to grow closer to God. It is what sustains me, and it is wonderful. I feel that closeness not just with my mind, but also in my heart and soul.

We are all touched by God. I believe we all feel God's presence, whether we are Christians or not. The Lord reaches out to us all, creating that conscious understanding that there is more to life than our mere existence on earth. There is only one Savior though. Jesus is the perfect way to understand that truth and to grasp God's love.

Our Christian faith enables us to begin to understand all that Jesus did for us on the cross. We are imperfect beings in an imperfect world, lost in our selfish tendencies, and drifting apart from that salvation Jesus has created for us. Without Jesus' loving sacrifice, we fall short of any meaningful relationship with God. We return to the imperfect earth from which we came. But that is not God's will.

As Christians, God loves us enough to bless us by residing within us. We are called through the Holy Spirit to embrace Jesus' sacrifice, glorify his name, share in that perfect communion of the Trinity, and invite others to join in as well. All three persons of God work together for all of us.

In The Lord's Prayer, Jesus asks us to pray to the Lord, "Thy will be done, on earth as it is in heaven." Heaven exists down here in you in the form of the Holy Spirit. God the Father, the Son, and Holy Spirit all want to commune with you more than anything: right now. In love, they have sacrificed everything in order to make that relationship possible.

But it is up to us to accept that glorious gift, to engage with the Holy Spirit in us, and to work with him to manifest our own faith and glorify his name. For me, this is where that "upward turn" begins.

These truths give me hope, and allow me to look to the future. It is also in restructuring and working through this grief that I understand these truths better. Recovery becomes a positive cycle. The more clearly I see where the meaning in our life comes from, the better I feel. And the more I lean into the love of God, the more thankful and grateful I become for that love.

That love was manifest in Jesus, but resides in us today as the Holy Spirit. For me, this is the "truth" that Jesus came to deliver, and that we are called on to demonstrate. Our communion with God is most important in that it enables us to express that love and community with others. That love and community has been the source of my recovery and is now my heaven on earth.

Jesus told us the Great Commandment in Matthew, Mark, Luke, and John. I paraphrase here: "You shall love the Lord your God with all your heart, and with all your soul, and with all your mind, and with all your strength. And you shall love your neighbor as yourself" (Mark 12:30–31).

For me, these words sound less like a commandment and more like a prescription for living. This is the way of the Trinity, and our best way to bring heaven down to earth. God's love was certainly given to me through the Spirit more than I was able to reciprocate. Sharing that love in ourselves with others is the other way to soak in God's presence.

As I move through the emotions of grief after Nathan's death, I see myself actually coming to a place of peace and even joy. God's peace was first given to me in the form of shock. Moving on, I felt it constantly from the signs of Nathan's salvation: from songs and psalms.

As I mentioned before, Taber had started college at Auburn during this traumatic fall for our family. The only thing that made Sarah and me comfortable sending him back was that he was returning to a fraternity full of "brothers" who cared for him incredibly through this ordeal.

An hour after we told Taber that Nathan was lost, he called back. He was confused, scared, and tearful. But in that short time, he was also surrounded by all fifty of his pledge brothers. They had congregated at their "house" and were crying alongside him. They did the work of pausing Taber's classes and getting him home to be with us. Being surrounded by others, especially as a loving community, often seems like the only way to counter the anguish death brings.

I am also determined not to repeat Nathan's mistakes in dealing with his depression. I have resolved not to suffer through this alone. For me, God's presence and love are manifest in all those around me.

I first felt at joy after Nathan's death at Auburn. I was visiting Taber for the Thanksgiving Iron Bowl (Auburn vs. Alabama) with my best friend whose daughter also attended Auburn. At Auburn, they take pride in being one big Auburn "family." When we entered the football stadium, that theme was spelled out across the stands by the band. It brought tears to my eyes.

The joy came as the game progressed, and Auburn closed out a 26-14 victory. Storming the field, surrounded by 100,000 elated people, I was able to forget the events of the last two months.

A year later, friends organized a weekend getaway in the mountains. Guys only. The weekend was full of the usual shenanigans, namely guns, bourbon, and camaraderie. I hardly thought of Nathan for three days. It was pure bliss.

The cycle of life, death, and resurrection, through God's grace, is manifest in me now, just as it has been in Jesus and Nathan. Too often we focus on the negatives in our society, and there are a lot of devastating negatives. But God has an immediate answer. Jesus is that answer. He has conquered death, and resurrection will be our ultimate reality someday.

As material things slip through your fingers, you tend to grasp at the spiritual. Nathan is gone in body, and it is only in spirit that he still lives on in our family. He no longer resides on this earth, but in the kingdom of God. "Blessed are the poor in spirit, for theirs is the kingdom of heaven. Blessed are those who mourn, for they shall be comforted" (Matthew 5:3-4) "Blessed are the pure in heart, for they shall see God" (Matthew 5:8).

I can tell you that it is easier to see this from the bottom.

I am not the first to suffer. We all become lost at times for many reasons. Of course, death will ultimately be part of all our lives. Even nature is proof that things turn around for the better though. The cycle of life is all around us.

Energy in our world is not lost but merely transformed. Rains bring water, forest fires cleanse, rot and decay provide food. Recessions recover, wars lead to reconciliation, and sorrow brings about love. Jesus said, "Unless a grain of wheat falls into the earth and dies, it remains alone; but if it dies, it bears much fruit" (John 12:24).

Winter becomes Spring. Death becomes life. For each of us, whether we suffer from death or depression, reconstruction and hope will come.

That hope for me comes from the Holy Spirit. He provides all the love and guidance we need. As Galatians 5:22–23 tells us, "The fruit of the Spirit is love, joy, peace, patience, kindness, goodness, faithfulness, gentleness, self-control."

Ultimately, this is where I find my greatest comfort these days.

Question: What brings you joy? How much time do you devote to this part of your life?

Action: Start a book club with a purpose (self-improvement, learning history, graphic novels, nature, doing good, charity, societal issues). My favorite books: *Love Does* by Bob Goff, *The Road Less Traveled* by M. Scott Peck, *The Killer Angels* by Michael Shaara, *The Forest Unseen* by David George Haskell, *The Soul of an Octopus* by Sy Montgomery, *The Selected Works of T. S. Spivet* by Relf Larsen, *The Book of Joy* by the Dalai Lama and Desmond Tutu, *Malcolm X* by Alex Haley, and *Waking up White, and Finding Myself in the Story of Race* by Debby Irving.

— 15 —

Binity Me

On the last night of his life, Jesus taught his disciples to pray, beginning with the words, "Our Father." Jesus was making clear that his Father in heaven was, indeed, father to us all. He was summing up the purpose of his ministry on earth: to include us all in the complete love of the Trinity.

Every one of us—every single human—is a lost sheep that God would journey through any wilderness to bring home. The most obvious example of this is Jesus' life earth and all he sacrificed to save us. But it also includes our own personal valleys of shadow and darkness. God is alongside us—actually within us—crying out to comfort us, yearning to teach us the truth of his love and our community with him.

At that last supper, Jesus also reminded the disciples of his spirit, whom he would send down to us after his death. He tells us in John 16:7: "I tell you the truth, it is to your advantage that I go away; for if I do not go away, the Helper will not come to you; but if I go, I will send Him to you."

Jesus again promises his spirit when he has been resurrected back to earth, "You will be baptized with the Holy Spirit not many days from now" (Acts 1:5). Indeed, shortly after Jesus ascends into heaven, the day of Pentecost arrives. "They [the disciples] were all filled with the Holy Spirit" (Acts 2:4).

Paul later refers to this indwelling Spirit in 1 Corinthians 3:16, "Do you not know that you are a temple of God and that the Spirit of God dwells in you?" There are two Greek words for temple used in the New Testament: *hieron* and *naos*. The *hieron* refers to the holy or hallowed ground and physical structures of the "temple," the entire area.

The *naos* is the inner sanctum of the temple, the "Holy of Holies." It is typically a place behind the pulpit separated by a curtain or wall where only the priests are allowed. When Jesus died, that is the curtain that was torn in half, opening up the inner sanctum to the world. The most holy place of the temple that was previously reserved for only the priests was opened up for all of us.

The New Covenant that Jesus establishes with his death is created for all of us: holy men and laypeople, Jews and Gentiles. Paul used the word *naos* to describe this resting place in us. We are literally the temple of God, the holiest of places in which God resides.

Another quote from Jesus references this in Mark 14:58, "I will destroy this temple made with hands, and in three days I will build another made without hands." God cherishes us above all else, so much so that he is willing to live with and within us. Our faith in him is rewarded with his Holy Spirit in us!

Nowadays, as I pray The Lord's Prayer, I am often by myself. Yet, I still begin with "Our Father" and not "My Father." For I never think of myself as alone anymore. The Spirit is with me. I am a we. "Our" is not at all inappropriate, because there are two of us praying together: me and the Spirit within me. I travel through this life now as two persons: myself and the Holy Spirit, a living binity.

Certainly, I am not divine and am not perfect in my relationship with the Spirit (as he exists within the Holy Trinity). But I do coexist with him. We are united as a pair. A binity. And I am no longer complete without him.

I must admit there is a part of me that is comforted by others' struggles. I can then better understand that I am not alone. This world is a community and the more I share in my pain with others, the less my pain becomes. More importantly, though, I am reminded of the "Footprints" poem, Psalm 23, and Lazarus' death—and that God is also suffering alongside me.

It is a beautiful thing to commune with God. To recognize that Spirit within us and understand his ways. Just as Jesus came down to earth—literally and figuratively tore open the alter curtains, and opened up God's covenant to all—he now pours his being, the Holy Spirit, into us all.

Remember that promise of Pentecost: "You will be baptized with the Holy Spirit" (Acts 1:5), and "You will receive power when the Holy Spirit has come upon you" (Acts 1:8). He is available to us all. Indeed, in faith, he already resides in us.

Furthermore, I consider it my role as a Christian to recognize the Spirit and allow him to guide my actions. I like the phrase "receive the Holy Spirit." As Christians, God has done his part. In fact, he keeps reaching out to us and works to get our attention. However, we often are too self-centered to recognize this.

The Spirit—God—is there, but it is now our job to reach out and "receive" him. Jeremiah puts it this way in chapter 29:13: "You will seek Me and find Me when you search for Me with all your heart." Jesus stated (Matthew 22:37, Mark 12:30, Luke 10:27), "Love the Lord your God with all your heart, and with all your soul, and with all your mind, and with all your strength."

This is our part to play in the New Covenant.

Question: Have you ever considered the Holy Spirit's role in your life? Do you ever slow down enough to listen to your conscience?

Action: Spend a weekend like a monk. Use any combination of the following to meditate physically and mentally on your needs and existence: fasting, solitude, simplicity, and silence.

___ 16 ___

Binity You

I n Luke 11:1–13, Jesus' disciples ask him how they should pray. Jesus first recites The Lord's Prayer to them. But he does not stop there. In his efforts to teach us to pray, he tells them a parable about a friend bringing "whatever he needs" when asked.

Jesus then spells out the moral of his story: "Ask, and it will be given to you; seek, and you will find; knock, and it will be opened to you. For everyone who asks, receives; and he who seeks, finds; and to him who knocks, it will be opened. Now suppose one of you fathers is asked by his son for a fish; he will not give him a snake instead of a fish, will he? Or if he is asked for an egg, he will not give him a scorpion, will he? If you then, being evil, know how to give good gifts to your children, how much more will your heavenly Father give the Holy Spirit to those who ask Him?"

This is a critical component to our prayers. It comes right after The Lord's Prayer in Jesus' teachings. Ask, and you shall receive. And when you ask, ask for the Holy Spirit.

Once you faithfully accept Jesus Christ as your savior and have faith in all that God the Father and the Son have done for you, the Holy Spirit resides in you. In John 7:38–39, Jesus says, "'He who believes in Me, as the Scripture said, From his innermost being will flow rivers of living water.' But this He spoke of the Spirit, whom those who believed in him were to receive."

Paul reiterated this in Romans 5:5, "The love of God has been poured out within our hearts through the Holy Spirit who was given to us." God's Spirit is physically in us!

David recognized this in his "valley of the shadow of death." It took that for me too. Sometimes we are so stubborn that we need to reach our lowest point to understand the need we have for God's peace and salvation.

C. S. Lewis (*The Problem of Pain*) said, "God whispers to us in our pleasures, speaks in our conscience, but shouts in our pain." This was certainly true for me. As low as my life became after Nathan's death, when nothing else mattered, it seemed like all that was left was the love of God.

I would go back to Adam and Eve. They had everything in the Garden of Eden. A perfect relationship with God, and all their needs were met. But Satan convinced them that they needed to taste evil to appreciate what was good. And now we are all left suffering similarly from this human frailty.

Evil exists, and God often uses it to direct us back to him. I pray that you will recognize that Garden of Eden that resides in a relationship with the Lord and his son, even here on earth, and that the Spirit is the bridge to such a relationship. Indeed, the Lord sets that table before us in the presence of our enemies. But that same banquet is there for us in good times as well. We just need to recognize that gift.

The Bible often describes people's relationship with the Holy Spirit as being "filled with the Spirit." We know God has done his part. The Spirit is there, filling us up. But do you recognize this? Do you allow it to happen? Do you allow your "cup to run over?"

If we can be filled, we can also be emptied. Too often the distractions and anxieties separate us from our relationship to God. Humbly submit yourself to the Lord, and he will fill you with his love. Resist all temptations of this world and seek his truth. Read the word and study it. Pray to him continuously, and let him walk beside you in your everyday actions, not just the worst of times.

Explore new ways to act on your faith and serve the Lord. Engage your community of believers to evaluate your own faith and actions. Do good works in ways that reflect a true understanding of the sacrifices Jesus Christ has made for you.

If you know that through Jesus you are saved, and through the Spirit you are provided all you need on this earth, and that in the end everything of this earth means nothing compared to the glories that await you in heaven, then reflect this faith in your everyday good works. Yes, you can be empty of your God, but you can also, through diligence, be "filled with the Spirit."

On the last night of his life, Jesus found himself alone with his Father in the Garden of Gethsemane. The disciples had all fallen asleep and left Jesus to face the impending hardships of the next day alone. Like us, he struggled with this role and the difficulties of the evils of our world. He demonstrated in that moment how we should deal with such trials—how we should surrender ourselves to God and learn to lean on the Spirit within us.

"My Father, if it is possible, let this cup pass from Me; yet not as I will, but as You will" (Matt 26:39). He prays similarly two more times before he is arrested, almost to convince his human self of God's righteous call, "Your will be done" (Matt 26:42). We, too, need to submit to the Spirit.

As you begin to walk with the Spirit through good times and bad, through trials and tribulations, your relationship and communion with the Trinity will become more obvious to you. Recognize that the Spirit walks with you in your daily life, and that relationship will become more personal and meaningful. You are a binity too. And God yearns to experience blessings, joy, love, pain, suffering, and growth with you. He aches to be part of your life. Reach out and receive this infinite gift!

Question: How often do you reflect on God? Only on Sundays? Daily? Never? Are your actions in this regard in line with your desires?

Action: Pray to the Holy Spirit. Ask him to reveal himself to you. Ask him to be part of your life. Ask him to help you through every aspect of your daily activities. Ask him to guide you toward growth and transformation in your relationship with the Trinity.

Epilogue 2

There is much hope in this world. That hope comes in the form of love. All of us are born with that capacity to love. To give it and to receive it.

Through my Christian lens, I see that internal, God-given love as the Holy Spirit. I also believe that the most perfect manifestation of that love is Jesus Christ.

And I believe that everyone can benefit from this realization.

The trials and tribulations of this world can ultimately only be overcome by this love, which is God.

This is the truth that Nathan's death has made so abundantly clear to me.

Part III—**The Holy Spirit**

17

A Sacred Home

The trinitarian God has been likened to water, which can exist in three forms: solid ice, liquid water, and gaseous steam. All three persons of the Trinity are the same God, but have different roles to play.

God the Father is our creator and judge. He is an infinitely powerful and all-knowing deity.

Jesus is the Son, God personified. He showed us who God is through the lens of his human form. Of course, Jesus is also our Savior. He lived a perfect life and died for our sins. This is immeasurably vital and the cornerstone of our Christian faith. It enables us to renew that perfect communion with God, and is a sacrifice for which we can only be humbly thankful.

The Holy Spirit is perhaps the most misunderstood and least known of the three. This is a tragedy in itself.

The Holy Spirit is actually the first person of the Trinity mentioned specifically in the Bible. That verse is Genesis 1:2, "The Spirit of God was moving over the surface of the waters." From the beginning, the Spirit has been that part of the Trinity that acts directly on earth.

In the creation, we see him as the one down on earth, doing the works the Father commands. Job 33:4 sums up the essential role of the Holy Spirit in our creation: "The Spirit of God has made me, and the breath of the Almighty gives me life."

The Holy Spirit is referenced 103 times throughout the Old Testament. He is often described as "filling" or "coming upon" the prophets, providing understanding, guidance, and divine inspiration ("in spirit").

Isaiah 11:2 describes him as "the spirit of wisdom and understanding, the spirit of counsel and strength, the spirit of knowledge and the fear of the Lord."

Even before our salvation is carried out in the form of Jesus Christ, the Holy Spirit was on earth, providing loving care and understanding to his unworthy creation.

In the Gospels (the first four books of the New Testament, the ones directly about Jesus' life on earth), we see how crucial the Holy Spirit is to Jesus' mission on earth. It is through the Holy Spirit that the virgin Mary conceives Jesus (Luke 1:35, "The Holy Spirit will come upon you . . . and for that reason the holy Child shall be called the Son of God.").

The Spirit is at Jesus' baptism (Matthew 3:16, "After being baptized, Jesus came up immediately from the water; and behold, the heavens were opened, and he saw the Spirit of God descending as a dove and lighting on Him."). After his baptism, Jesus is "led around by the Spirit in the wilderness for forty days" (Luke 4:1). He is unsuccessfully tempted by the devil, and returns to begin his ministry. "And Jesus returned to Galilee in the power of the Spirit . . . And He began teaching in their synagogues and was praised by all" (Luke 4:14–15).

From then on the Holy Spirit is with Jesus, providing comfort, guidance, and understanding. Jesus explains it this way, "The words that I say to you I do not speak on My own initiative, but the Father abiding in Me [the Holy Spirit] does His works" (John 14:10).

Throughout his life, Jesus seemed to tap into a higher power. He was intimately connected to his Father and through him performed many miracles, modeled a perfect love, and showed us who God is himself and what he desires for us. Jesus continuously prayed to his Father, sought solitude with him, and showed him his heart. In his own words, he achieved all this through the power of the Holy Spirit.

Imagine what it would mean to have that power at your disposal.

After Jesus' crucifixion, Jesus is resurrected to earth and appears to the disciples. "He presented himself alive after His suffering, by many convincing proofs, appearing to them over a period of forty days and speaking of the things concerning the kingdom of God" (Acts 1:3).

At the end of this period, Jesus made a promise to the disciples, "You will be baptized with the Holy Spirit not many days from now" (Acts 1:5). Indeed, about a week after Jesus permanently ascends to heaven, the day of Pentecost arrives.

The Holy Spirit arrives on earth permanently at Pentecost (Pentecost literally means "50," as in 50 days after Jesus died). The Spirit's arrival is beyond anything the apostles had expected, even though Jesus had fully explained the power and significance of the Spirit's arrival.

Acts 2:2–4 says, "And suddenly there came from heaven a noise like a violent rushing wind, and it filled the whole house where they were sitting. And there appeared to them tongues as of fire distributing themselves, and they rested on each one of them. And they were all filled with the Holy Spirit."

Notice the Holy Spirit does not come to earth and stand alone physically as Jesus did. The Holy Spirit comes and immediately "fills" himself into the apostles. He arrives to guide the apostles in their faith and ministry. Their immediate ability to speak all languages enabled them to travel the world and spread the word of God.

In Jesus' Great Commission in Mark 16:15–18, he describes the power this gives them. "Go into all the world and preach the gospel to all creation . . . These signs will accompany those who have believed: in My name they will cast out demons, they will speak with new tongues, they will pick up serpents, and if they drink any deadly poison, it will not hurt them; they will lay hands on the sick, and they will recover."

From then on, the power of the Holy Spirit—the power of God—was with the apostles.

The Holy Spirit is referred to 247 times in the New Testament. Fifty-one of those times are in the Gospels, as the Spirit guides Jesus through his work on earth. The remaining 196 times are in the Book of Acts and the apostles' letters that follow (after Pentecost). These instances reveal how ever-present and vital the Spirit was to the apostles—to the earliest Christians—in their every actions. Peter, Paul, James (Jesus' brother), and John among them.

They all include the Spirit (and take heed to mention him specifically) in every meeting, decision, and action they take. They understood and lived in intimate relationship with God and allowed his will to be done through them. The meaning of Jesus' life and the crux of our own Christianity was revealed through the power of the Spirit in them. The Spirit gave them the guidance, strength, and wisdom to enable the church to grow and thrive against all odds.

Even personally, to each one of those patriarchs of our faith, the Spirit was vital to their faith and good works. And today, the Spirit is just as alive in us, working to connect us to God our Father and Jesus. Enabling us, as much as we allow, to grow in faith and spread the message of love and salvation.

I believe we can perform miracles (perhaps not as dramatic as handling snakes or surviving poison). Every day people learn new languages, connect to each other, heal the sick, and commit to their faith in God and Jesus. The critical point, though, is to whom do we ascribe this power.

Unfortunately, Pentecost and the importance of the Holy Spirit gets lost for many of us generally and specifically. Pentecost becomes just another vague time in the church calendar. We ignore the importance of the Holy Spirit.

Actually, I'm willing to bet many of us don't even notice when Pentecost comes each year (hopefully you now understand it's fifty days after Easter). Of course, Jesus is our Savior. He is the only reason we are able to have an intimate relationship with God in the first place. But just as Jesus serves as a perfect physical example of God's love, the Holy Spirit maintains that truth within us spiritually.

The Spirit is at work in us just as much as he was with the apostles. He continually glorifies Jesus' works and provides us with that inspiration to return to the Lord. As often as we wander away in our lives, without the Spirit's persistence we'd remain lost. Without him, in our human selfishness, we'd likely forget that Jesus existed at all. The Holy Spirit is our personal shepherd.

Remember Jesus' words at The Last Supper: "It is to your advantage that I go away; for if I do not go away, the Helper will not come to you; but if I go, I will send Him to you" (John 16:7).

We've explored how the word *parakletos* describes how the Spirit "comforts" us in our times of need. But it can also be used to show how the Spirit "helps" us understand the truth of Christianity, experience a complete spiritual communion with God, and work toward glorifying his name in our words and deeds.

I contend that as gloriously joyous as Christmas is in celebrating the birth of Jesus on this earth, Pentecost should be equally celebrated as the permanent arrival of God on earth, in you. Celebrate the coming of the Holy Spirit into your life today.

Jesus stands in word and life as the manifestation of God and our Savior. Studying the Gospels is critical to understanding Jesus' life and God's love.

But God is also physically present with you today. The Holy Spirit is just as vital to your grasping the love of God. Just as the Spirit was given to the disciples on Pentecost, he is a gift to us all now. He is our current link to God. His love, his presence in our lives is the best chance we have to understanding God at all— growing in our faith along the way, and appreciating the sacrifice Jesus made for us.

How great is that? It means that the whole of the kingdom of heaven is at our ready disposal.

Question: Do you believe you are fundamentally good or bad? What is our true nature?

Action: Read a religious book. My favorites: *The Jesus I Never Knew* by Philip Yancey, *The Universal Christ* by

Richard Rohr, *The Reason for God* by Timothy Keller, *The Screwtape Letters* by C. S. Lewis, *The Holy Spirit: An Introduction* by John Bevere, *Transforming Presence* by Daniel Henderson, *Forgotten God* by Francis Chan, and *How to Be Filled with the Holy Spirit* by A.W. Tozer.

18

A Kingdom Life

I n my grief, I have learned to look at how God handles evil. He does not manipulate it as often as we would like. Jesus makes this point clear from the beginning when the devil tempts him. Jesus began his ministry by rejecting sustenance, miracles, and power for the sake of freedom.

God allows us our freedoms on earth. This freedom comes with the pitfalls of being human. Our world is full of conscious evil brought about in it. It is also full of unconscious and random imperfections. Death and despair are regular companions for many of us. But so is righteousness, love, and life. Freedom gives us the power to choose. And there is nothing more powerful than the choice to love.

I refuse to believe God chose to have Nathan die so that some more profound good could come of it. Nothing, it seems to me, could compensate for such overwhelming loss. Of course, I do not understand the mysterious ways of God. It is equally hard for me to fully comprehend the glories of heaven that overwhelm such suffering. But small glimpses still abound and often come about despite such tragedies.

My loss is such a small fraction of what others experience every day. Surely you have experienced your own losses. God allows many tragedies to happen. But he also loves us greatly, yearns to be with us, and chooses to walk alongside us during all this good and bad. If Jesus Christ can suffer as much as any human being has, then certainly we are not immune either.

One of the most faithful prayers in the Bible comes in the Old Testament book of Daniel. Three Jewish men—Shadrach, Meshach, and Abednego—are about to be thrown into a fiery furnace, put to death for their devotion to their god.

Given one last chance to renounce their faith and bow down and worship the king's god, they refuse the evil king: "O Nebuchadnezzar, we have no need to answer you in this matter. If this be so, our God whom we serve is able to deliver us from the burning fiery furnace, and he will deliver us out of your hand, O king. But if not, be it known to you, O king, that we will not serve your gods" (Dan 3:16–18).

The most remarkable element of this prayer to me is not that the men know their god can deliver them from the fiery furnace, but that they declare—even if he does not—this will not change their faith in him. Our prayers are not always answered in the ways we desire. We would do well to follow the example of these three men and know that whatever happens, God will deliver us out of the fires of this world and into his loving kingdom. Nothing can stand in the way of that.

Of course, when Shadrach, Meshach, and Abednego are thrown into the furnace, the fire has no power over them. Walking in the midst of the fire, the king now sees four men. "The appearance of the fourth is like a son of the gods" (Dan 3:25). The fourth man is the Son of God. Jesus never abandons us, no matter how terrible our fiery furnace. He is with us always, delivering us from this world's troubles.

I am aware now more than ever that death is part of this world. We all will be touched by death many times in our lives. At the very least, we will have to come to grips with our own death.

Of course, having a child die—and die by suicide—brings its own emotions that make one's recovery especially challenging. Feelings of what might have been for Nathan as well as my own guilt and shame compound my deep sorrow. I have been through every circumstance and scenario of his death many times over. I relive this pain daily.

Emotionally, I am not equipped to handle this despair on my own. As a pediatrician, what good was all my studying if I could not even save my son? What good are my prayers if God does not answer them? Why rest in his arms if it just brings death and destruction?

It is impossible for our puny, human minds to grasp his overall plan. We are too small and self-centered to see though our own troubles. Neither are we strong enough to tolerate the injustices brought upon us. Thankfully, God is not of this world. The kingdom of God is so much bigger than all this. Spiritually, we have all the help we need.

On earth, all we can do is choose to respond to such tragedy with God and lean on him to carry us through to a greater glory. Jesus conquered death, but before that he had to die. During his life, he suffered alongside us. And now, during our struggles, he still suffers with us.

At Lazarus' tomb, he cried at the sadness of his death, right before he was to raise him from the dead. God responds to all our sadness with the same tears. And then prepares a banquet for us among our enemies.

God responds with a vigorous love that can overcome whatever we are going through. When we learn to let go of this life and give it over to God, we begin to see that his steady hand is all we can rest in—and that is very good.

So much of Nathan's last year—his suffering and death—is still painful to me. I do not feel at home in this world, and for me there has been only one way to turn. Today it is so much easier to lose myself in the wonders of God's love than to dwell on the pain of this world. I can imagine Nathan's peace and yearn to hug my son again.

So what is this place of peace that I seek out so often. It is a continuous theme in the Bible. It is the kingdom of God. Also referred to as the kingdom of Israel, of David, the Lord, and heaven and referenced throughout. For me, it is more real than what befalls me on this earth.

Christian denominations (and Judaism) debate on a specific definition for this kingdom. As narrow-minded humans, we place too many limitations on God. Just as the Trinity is a difficult concept for us to understand (God existing as one person, but in different ways), the kingdom of God exists infinitely beyond our understandings of time and space. It is far greater and more complex than we can possibly comprehend.

As a start, let us imagine the kingdom of God through the eyes of God. After all, he is a perfect reference point. Through the lens of the Father, the kingdom can be viewed as the universe. It is the physical place that the Lord created and rules over. From Jesus' point of view, he is the kingdom. John the Baptist referring to Jesus declared (and Jesus later reiterated), "Repent, for the kingdom of heaven is at hand" (Mat 4:17).

At least we understand that Jesus is the manifestation of God's divine sovereignty, come to restore his kingdom on earth.

If Jesus is the beginning of the kingdom on earth, then the Holy Spirit through us is the continuation of it. Paul understood this when he stated, "For the kingdom of God is not eating and drinking [of earthly things], but righteousness and peace and joy in the Holly Spirit" (Rom 14:17).

Jesus compared the kingdom of God to a mustard seed: "and this is smaller than all other seeds, but when it is full grown, it is larger than the garden plants and becomes a tree" (Matt 13:31–32). Indeed, this kingdom now grows through and in us.

The kingdom is also seen in the Book of Revelation as a place of the future, as an eventual heaven on earth where the Father, Son, and Holy Spirit come together permanently. Eventually, "The kingdom of the world has become the kingdom of our Lord and of His Christ, and He will reign forever and ever" (Rev 11:15).

For me, the most relevant realization of the kingdom is of that holy place that exists in me through the Holy Spirit. It is the freedom that is realized by the saving grace of Jesus, the living communion with other people, the peace of heaven in my soul, and the joy in knowing what is to come.

With God as our Father, Jesus as our Savior, and the Spirit as our Guide, we can cultivate our relationship with the Trinity and bring some of God's kingdom here on earth. When Jesus teaches us to pray in The Lord's Prayer, "Our Father, who is in heaven, hallowed be thy name. Thy kingdom come, thy will be done, on earth as it is in heaven," we are inviting God into our soul.

We are also acknowledging our role in actively bringing his kingdom down to earth. We know eventually God will do this for us. When Jesus arrives a second time, he will "wipe away every tear," and right every wrong. However, God wants us to realize his glory here today.

As Christians, it is our commission to foster his kingdom—his will—here on earth. Through the Holy Spirit, we are given everything we need. God is with you—not in spirit—but in Spirit! His person is within you. Here to guide us toward a perfect communion with him. He is here to explain the Bible to us. To reveal all that Jesus is. To answer our prayers. To show us the way to a Christian life. And reveal God's glory to us and to help us glorify God to others.

That kingdom begins with God. God within us. Jesus showed us what it is like to be filled with the Spirit: "He is also the head of the body, the church; and He is the beginning, the firstborn from the dead, so that He Himself will come to have first place in everything" (Col 1:18). Most importantly, "love the Lord your God."

And extend the kingdom of God to your relationships with others: "Love your neighbor as yourself" (Mat 19:19). See the Spirit in all of us. He is there too. We are all created in his image, and we all can tap into this heavenly perfection through the Spirit. Live in love. And grow in peace. Your heaven is here and now, on earth.

How do I know this? How can I be so sure? Because the kingdom of God is not a one-way street. I pray, and my prayers are answered. I cry, and my feelings are comforted. I am lost, but ultimately peace in my life is restored. I know the Holy Spirit is with me at every moment.

Question: Dr. Martin Luther King Jr. stated: "Every man lives in two realms: the internal and the external. The internal is that realm of spiritual ends expressed in art, literature, morals, and religion. The external is that complex of devices, techniques, mechanisms, and instrumentalities by means of which we live." Which world do you live in?

Action: Watch an inspirational video on Consecration:

Denzel Washington: https://www.youtube.com/watch?v=--1dFvyjt-A

Billy Graham: https://www.youtube.com/watch?v=GR68pzuC7TU

Matthew Stevenson: https://www.youtube.com/watch?v=UNo-DhBEywE

Leoneida Padilla: https://www.youtube.com/watch?v=OTH2_zmUhNw

19

Divine Revelations

H ope actually seems like too weak a word for me these days. It connotes too much uncertainty about the future. Much as my faith has become more of a knowledge about God's existence and Nathan's salvation, my emotions about these facts are much more than just hoping it is true.

At this point, joy is probably too strong a word though. I am content to settle on peace as the state of my mind. Just as Nathan is at peace in heaven, I feel the Holy Spirit has brought me peace on earth. The emptiness in my heart that is left by Nathan's passing is beginning to be filled with promise, understanding, and love.

Two things make me certain that God is reaching down through the Holy Spirit to Sarah and me during these terrible days, weeks, months, and years after our son's death. One is the frequency and timing of the messages we receive. Early on, I can remember speaking to Sarah about it. We would relate to each other that just as we prayed for a sign, it would arrive.

The other thing that gives me confidence in God's presence is the relevance of the messages we received. The power and specificity of God's words—the way he constantly opens up his heart to us, showering us with his love—surely is no coincidence.

Nathan's number on the football team was 42. He had just transferred schools, and so this was a new number for him; we tried to find meaning in it. There are not many famous football players who wore the number. Ronnie Lott came to mind, but

Nathan surely did not remember a San Francisco 49er from the eighties and nineties.

In baseball, Jackie Robinson wore 42. This was significant, and Nathan knew it. During Taber's confirmation, our bishop had preached about Jackie Robinson as the movie "42" had just come out. He spoke of Jackie's strength of character and his perseverance in the face of terrible racism. He also spoke of his tremendous faith that gave him the courage to withstand many of the torments he endured. From that day on, we all celebrated Jackie's achievements and faith.

Taber, Nathan, and I got vintage "Jersey City" baseball caps to honor the first professional team Jackie Robinson played for. But for us, the "JC" on the caps represented Jesus Christ. On the day I gave the boys their hats, we sat down to dinner and discussed the incredible love and gift those hats represented. It is a hat I still proudly wear.

On the night Nathan's body was found, his football team was playing a game. He had been lost for four days at that point, and the team had "42" stickers on the backs of their helmets in an effort to rally the community toward finding him safe.

As the news came in, the community was in shock, and the team was devastated. Sarah and I were home and were truly overwhelmed. A terrible week of searching had ended in an unimaginable and horrific way, and now we were lost.

As devastated as we were, we were also comforted by God's grace and Nathan's salvation. Lost in our shock, two days later we were at a candlelight vigil for Nathan, sitting up in the balcony, undetected. The service was meant for his peers to help them grapple with this trauma before the actual funeral. I did not hear a word of it.

My only thought was *Why?* In my muddled mind, it was not even a prayer. It was just my state of being. What I did not realize in that fog was that God was listening.

Afterward, everyone stood quietly outside, not knowing quite how to comfort each other. We found ourselves among them, sharing hugs and empty sympathies. Sarah ended up surrounded by the football team, the only light in the area shining down on her. From where I stood, it seemed as if she was actually preaching to them.

"Nathan is not really gone," she said, looking into each of their heartbroken faces. "He is still in all of our hearts; he lives with all of you, and he is present with us now. You will see, this week you will go out and score 42 points and win your game. You will know he is with you."

It was a difficult week for the team, but they played a game the next Friday against an undefeated team three hours away in Charlestown. They still had their "42" stickers on their helmets. At halftime, they were ahead 28-10. As the second half progressed, Sarah's phone began to light up from texts from the parents who had made it to the game. "Do you see what is happening?" "I can't believe this!" "They scored again!" "It's now 42-10, but there are still seven minutes left!"

The next time we heard from them was a phone call from one of the mothers. She was on the field with everyone else, celebrating a miraculous 42-10 victory! She handed the phone to the head coach. "I don't know what happened," he said. "We weren't trying to score 42 points!"

Many of the players were in tears, just as they had been at that candlelight vigil, and just as they had been at Nathan's funeral. These were not tears of sadness; they were tears of unbelievable revelation, of a recognition that higher powers were at work, and that perhaps there was a greater story at play for all of us.

It was truly a joyful moment, and the first glimpse that maybe Nathan's death might actually serve a larger purpose. That from all this depression, hopelessness, and death, God was at work, creating a blessing from such a tragedy. Perhaps some good could come from Nathan's death. That good was his salvation, and just maybe that message would be understood by others.

Shortly thereafter, someone told us to ask Alexa, "What is the meaning of life?" The answer she will give you even today is 42. The answer is sort of a joke. Like so many random questions and answers you can ask Alexa, the creators of her program must have had a lot of fun designing creative ways to entertain us. You can ask her how old Santa is, or what her favorite food is, etc. But 42 as the meaning of life?

It is a reference to the book, *The Hitchhikers Guide to the Galaxy.* The book is a satire, where earth is destroyed, and the lone survivor searches the universe for the meaning of life. In the end, his answer comes from a supercomputer designed by a race of super-intelligent beings. The computer spits out the answer, a seemingly random 42.

However, in the computer language ASCII (the author, Douglas Adams was a major computer nerd), the number 42 represents an asterisk. Furthermore, in computer programing, an asterisk is often used to symbolize "Whatever you want it to be." And so, Alexa's answer to the question "What is the meaning of life?" is really, "Whatever you want it to be."

In Nathan's case, what we wanted and where our hearts constantly turned was back to God.

The number 42 has come up in many meaningful ways since. It doesn't always answer my Why? prayer. But it always reminds me how God responds to evil and death. It reminds me of Nathan's peace in salvation. It comforts me to know he is well.

HUGS is an organization that cares for those who have lost a loved one to suicide. It was started in 2001 by a mother who lost her own son to suicide at sixteen years old, the same age as Nathan. Her son's picture on the HUGS website pictures him in his football uniform. His number was also 42.

Nathan was a huge Marvel movie fan. We were all looking forward to seeing the upcoming movie *Thor: Ragnarok* and had our tickets preordered before he died. Sarah, Elle Louise, and I went anyway—without him. His empty seat seemed to symbolize our permanent loss.

I prayed a lot at that movie, feeling the emptiness without him. It seemed to me at that point that there were better things for him to do in heaven, but I asked Nathan anyway to please let us know that he was with us on that night.

One of the main characters in the movie is identified as Scrapper 142, and the theme music for that movie was by Led Zeppelin, once again giving us the sense of Nathan's presence.

On his birthday, we went to see *Solo*. Harrison Ford was Nathan's favorite actor, and he would have wanted to see this movie as well. One of our friends quickly let us know that Harrison Ford was actually born in 1942. Another "random coincidence."

Our first vacation without Nathan was to Playa del Carmen in Mexico. Sarah, Elle Louise, and I went to play golf and were given two carts. Sarah sat in one cart alone, a vacant seat next to her where Nathan should have been. Elle Louise was the one who realized 42 was the number of the cart she was driving. It was one more reminder that Nathan is alive and well in heaven. God and him never really left and are still with us during our time here on earth.

Most illuminating was the time my friend and I, his son, and Elle Louise visited Nathan's grave at our church in preparation for his son's confirmation. The lesson we were solemnly discussing that day was death, Jesus' sacrifice for us, and our salvation through him. I also let them know how the Holy Spirit makes us aware of all of this.

We spoke of the song "Stairway to Heaven" and the number 42. We saw how Nathan's ashes are actually buried in the middle of a garden bed, exactly 42 bricks from either side. I tried to let them know how the Lord speaks to us—sometimes subtly, sometimes more directly—but that he is always there, looking over us. Many of these concepts were hard for the twelve year olds to process, but it was important to me that they hear this message.

The next night, God spoke louder and clearer than I ever could. Elle Louise was invited to the local minor league baseball game with her best friend. We hadn't been to a game in nearly two years, but this was a fun and relaxing way for her to get her mind off everything she was going through.

That night happened to be "Jackie Robinson Night." In honor of Jackie Robinson, the number 42 is retired from all teams in baseball. No one ever wears that number, except on this night. Every player on the field—for both teams—was wearing 42.

Elle Louise looked at the lineup on the scoreboard and says she thought she was going crazy. It was 42's up and down the lineup and all over the field! It was immediately obvious to her that God was present, and that Nathan was in good hands. Amazingly, God showed up again, making clear to my daughter that he was with her, and that Nathan, too, was still around.

In moments of human weakness, I wonder if this could all be true. Does God really speak to us through the Holy Spirit? Is he really working within us constantly to help us understand all God gives us, and to help glorify his name in and through us? Or are our minds powerful enough to play tricks on us?

Is shock, as the first stage of grief, a gift from God or just a psychological defense mechanism? As certainly as we need reassurances from God, does our mind just subconsciously create these opportunities for us to rationalize a convenient truth and help us cope? Perhaps my strong feelings are just a means for me to deal with such an unthinkable tragedy. Doubt creeps in.

I certainly do not begin to know all that God has to offer us. A certain amount of faith is necessary to hand over our salvation to God. It is important to trust him, so that we can be free to humbly serve him and extend his love to others.

Still, sometimes I like to fall back on my scientific background. I lean on the certainty of mathematics to show me what I cannot see. For instance, did Nathan just randomly pick the shirt he wore out the door on October 9, the one with that Led Zeppelin angel on it, that fallen, agonizing human turned angel? Or did God compel him to wear it for our sake, to point us toward the song "Stairway to Heaven" and all it symbolizes to us now?

How can it be just coincidence, all the specific ways the "Stairway to Heaven" lyrics relate to his story and our understanding of it? Nathan had about 25 t-shirts in his drawer that day, so I guess the chances we just got lucky were one in twenty-five. I suppose it is possible then that this was coincidence. Unlikely, but possible.

When I wonder about Jackie Robinson Night at the ballpark, it brings me back to my college statistics class. Consider the odds of my daughter going to the Knight's baseball game on Jackie Robinson

Day, on the day after we spent time specifically praying over his grave about the significance of that number in Nathan's death, and the message of his peaceful salvation it symbolized to us.

The chances of Nathan having Jackie Robinson's 42 are one in ninety-nine.

What about us praying over his grave the night before that game? I had had that specific conversation with my daughter three times in the year after Nathan's death (three in 365 nights). And she went to just that one Knights game that summer, so the chances that game was right after we'd spoken is one in 152 (the length of the Knights' season).

The chance that home game was Jackie Robinson Night, one out of seventy home games. So what are the chances that I speak to my daughter about Nathan's number 42, and the next night she attends a baseball game where all the players are wearing that exact number? Those odds are three in 99x365x152x70, or one in 128,158,800. That's one in 128 million!

Sometimes in my human misgivings, science shows me the overwhelming odds that God is at work in my life.

I bet you have your own miracles to tell. These are not coincidences. They are your own personal connection to God, which defies the odds. It is God speaking to you, right here on earth. To me it is analytical proof that God—his Spirit—is reaching out to us all. He is reminding us of his significance in our lives, and showing us that he is taking care of us all, Nathan included.

He reminded my daughter directly of his compassion for all those things Nathan's 42 symbolizes. On that night, he acknowledged his concern for Nathan, his covenant with all of us, his love for us, and our salvation through his son, Jesus Christ. If that seems like a stretch to you, I'm willing to bet at least 128 million to one that it is true. All emotions aside, those are pretty great odds.

I am sure that the depth of my sorrow has led to the need for an equally extreme response on God's part. He has shouted to me in our despair and reached down constantly to pull me up out of my misery. I can tell you it is easier to see his purpose from the bottom. As material things slip through your fingers, you tend to grasp at the spiritual.

Nathan is gone in body, and it is only his spirit that still lives on in our family. He no longer resides on this earth, but in the kingdom of God. "Blessed are the poor in spirit, for theirs is the kingdom of heaven." "Blessed are those who mourn, for they shall be comforted" (Mat 5:4). "Blessed are the pure in heart, for they shall see God" (Mat 5:8).

These statements make me think of Nathan as well as my family. God has reached us through the evils that have befallen our family.

However, I would like to believe it is not necessary to withstand such tragedy in order to commune with God on a spiritual level. It is best to prepare your mind, heart, and soul before such evils befall you. Not only so that you may better survive these trials, but also so that you can experience the joy and peace of a loving God throughout life, in good times and in bad.

This is my wish for you, and the message that I hope Nathan's death and my experiences convey.

Of course, this level of understanding is not attainable on your own. Spiritual disciplines and Bible study will only get you so far. It is a gradual process to grow in faith, and it is a difficult one.

As obvious as it sounds and as intuitive as it should be, God needs to be the first (and last) part of this process. And the most integral influence from God on earth is the Holy Spirit. I believe the Holy Spirit was the one reaching down to touch and comfort Sarah and me when Nathan died.

He was the one moving us toward the song "Stairway to Heaven" and Psalm 23. He was with Nathan's football team in their recovery. He showed my daughter how great is his love. He still constantly reminds me of Nathan's salvation. He does this through the number 42. Through science and math. And through others.

God's Spirit is our comforter, guide, and teacher. This is the needed power we have to tap into in order to truly experience, appreciate, and benefit from a complete community with God.

Paul described it thus: "Let no one boast in men. For all things belong to you, whether . . . the world or life or death or things present or things to come; all things belong to you, and you belong to Christ; and Christ belongs to God" (1 Cor 3:21–23).

I often seek refuge in the kingdom of God where I find God's Spirit. And when I get lost, God brings his kingdom to me. He showers me with reminders of his love. I have felt his presence.

Within his heavenly kingdom on earth, everything seems certain, known, makes sense, and is infinitely more real to me than the wrongs that exist by their side. On this earth, sometimes everything seems wrong. But through God's love, manifest as Jesus Christ and made evident through the Holy Spirit, everything is possible. To me, nothing can replace the safety, security, and peace of that certainty. I hope the importance of that statement is apparent to you.

Paul also taught us in Galatians 5:22–23, "The fruit of the Spirit is love, joy, peace, patience, kindness, goodness, faithfulness, gentleness, self-control."

As I move through the stages of grief after Nathan's death and grow in my relationship with God, I see myself actually arriving at that place of peace and sometimes even joy.

Question: What miracles have you witnessed in your life? How long did that sense of wonder at what you'd experienced last?

Action: Be a miracle to someone else. Pray for the Spirit to present you with an opportunity to be aware of someone else's needs, and then provide that need for them unasked.

20

Our Treasures on Earth

B ack before Nathan died, the Holy Spirit was elusive to me. As you read the Bible, however, it is impossible not to come across him. He fills the prophets throughout the Old Testament. Jesus was baptized in the Spirit. He walked in the Spirit. And he sent the Spirit to the apostles on Pentecost.

The Holy Spirit is critical to Jesus' ministry and to the apostles in forming the early church. Throughout the Bible, the Spirit is often seen "resting within," "coming upon," "poured into," and "filling" those of faith.

Most of my life, I have waited for some dramatic moment when the Spirit would unmistakably come upon me. I thought when God recognized my faith in him, he would let me know. I prayed for and anticipated my own personal burning bush or "Road to Damascus" moment. Maybe God would open the heavens, and the Spirit would literally descend like a dove upon me. I had reservations about the strength of my faith if I had not felt this obvious baptism.

Alas, the heavens have not opened up for me, at least literally. I cannot speak in tongues like the apostles. As a pediatrician, I cannot cure cancer or prevent every death in my patients. I could not save my own son. Perhaps I am not worthy. The Spirit is so difficult to grasp.

Of course, now I know better. The Spirit is already here. He always has been. Just as Jesus came down to earth, literally and figuratively tore open the alter curtains, and opened up God's covenant to all, he now pours his being—the Holy Spirit—into me.

Perhaps Nathan's death was my Road to Damascus. It is a terrible valley that I would not want for anyone. But in my pain, God has healed me. Did I need to be blinded before I could see?

Remember that promise on Pentecost, "You will be baptized with the Holy Spirit" (Acts 1:5), and "You will receive power when the Holy Spirit has come upon you" (Acts 1:8)? This is God's New Covenant, and it will never be broken. Know that God is already with you. His spirit has already come upon you.

This is my new reality. As I recognize his presence, revere his grace, and work toward getting to know him in mind and soul, he responds. In your spiritual practices, the Spirit will reveal himself in you too. And you will begin to understand fully the beauty of the Trinity.

How do we know the Spirit is filling us up? We first make this apparent in our actions. Jesus was the first to state that we would know him—and his Father—through his own good works. John 10:38 says, "Believe the works, so that you may know and understand that the Father is in Me, and I in the Father."

In Acts, we hear this message again, "Jesus of Nazareth, a man attested to you by God with miracles and wonders and signs which God preformed through Him in your midst" (Acts 2:22).

In this same way, we reflect Jesus' love and character when we do good. As Jesus proclaims, "Let your light shine before men in such a way that they may see your good works, and glorify your Father who is in heaven" (Matt 5:16).

And in John 3:21, "He who practices the truth comes to the Light, so that his deeds may be manifested as having been wrought in God." And finally at The Last Supper, "Truly, truly, I say to you, whoever believes in Me, the works that I do, he will do also; and greater works than these he will do" (John 14:12).

In loving God, we learn to shine his light to others. This graces them with your service, it blesses you with their gratitude, and ultimately, it glorifies God. God's goodness becomes readily apparent to you, and radiates from you. The Spirit is already in you. You need to take the next step in letting him shine forth.

Secondly, we will know the Spirit—and the Father and the Son—by their effects on us. Galatians 5:22–23 says, "The fruit of the Spirit is love, joy, peace, patience, kindness, goodness, faithfulness, gentleness, self-control."

The Holy Spirit, in a time of tragedy for me and my family, has been the great Comforter. Indeed, we have felt his peace. But this is only the beginning. The Spirit is so much more. Remember Jesus not only referred to the Spirit as our Helper/Comforter, but also as the "Spirit of Truth." In knowing God intimately—spiritually—we will also realize all the benefits of his kingdom.

Listen to Paul, "For the kingdom of God is not eating and drinking, but righteousness and peace and joy in the Holy Spirit" (Rom 14:17). And again in Romans 8:6, "For the mind set on the flesh is death, but the mind set on the Spirit is life and peace."

Paul seems to speak to us of the great glories that come from knowing the Lord: "Kindle afresh the gift of God . . . For God has not given us a spirit of timidity, but of power and love and discipline" (2 Tim 1:6–7).

I often begin my days now with a prayer that the Spirit will make his presence known to me today. I pray that in each moment, he will remind me that he is there and help me act as he wills. I pray that I will get out of his way. That I will extol his encompassing presence in every small step that the day brings.

Not long ago, I found myself at a gas station. On the other side of the pump, a woman was having trouble and not being quiet about it. I asked God if this was an opportunity for me to act for him. She disappeared to argue in the store. But when she returned, she was still upset. Evidently, her ten dollars of gas was not registering on her pump. Now that it was in the cash register and she had filled a complaint, the money would have to be mailed back to her. Maybe.

And so I hesitantly approached her. I pumped ten dollars of gas into her car with my credit card and offered her my simple prayer. "God bless you," I said as I walked away. And then she hugged me and thanked me for my kindness. We left acknowledging that God had indeed blessed us all. I felt good about the small part I had played. I felt joy in my heart.

A week later, I needed gas again. As I pulled up to the station and went to put my card in the pump, I noticed someone had left a card up against the small TV screen. It was a gift card and on it was written in pen "$10." I plugged it into the pump and gladly received my free ten dollars' worth of gas. God was with me and glad too. It was good.

With Sarah, my joy now comes in small, simple doses. It is as if we are starting over, rebuilding our relationship from the ground up. As such, I seem to have a greater understanding of what is meaningful between us. I find joy in just relaxing with her. My heart swells with her vulnerability, playfulness, and moments of laughter. Our love is more complete in our shared union, rather than just a complex of fragile emotions.

My faith started as a simple belief in God. With Nathan's death, it has evolved into a knowledge—an absolute certainty—in God's existence. Then it moved into a desire to know God more. And finally, I rest in the peace of knowing that God is love. That this love is the only reliable constant in this world and the next.

I can imagine Paul's statement on the fruits of the Spirit as a self-fulfilling prophesy. The more we act with the Spirit in mind, the more the Spirit acts in us.

Jesus said: "If I cast out demons by the Spirit of God, then the kingdom of God has come upon you . . . The good man brings out of his good treasure what is good" (Matt 12:28, 35).

Cast out your own demons. Be a good person. It is okay to start simply, with self-control, and kindness. To just learn that the more you give, the more you receive. Remember, too, the more you strive to get to know God and act out the love he's given you, the more you will realize the treasures in his kingdom. This is the true path to peace and joy. This is your heaven on earth.

The Holy Spirit is a tremendous gift from God. One that Jesus even touted was better for us than his staying on this earth. Indeed, without the Spirit, there is no understanding of God, no relationship with him, and ultimately no life within our souls. It is in our Binity, which God teaches us to become part of the perfect, selfless relationship of servitude that is the Trinity God.

The truth is that in spreading God's love to others, we come to realize the glories of all that God intends for us.

Question: Which of the fruits of the Spirit (love, joy, peace, patience, kindness, goodness, faithfulness, gentleness, self-control) do you relate to the most? Which do you relate to the least? Which one does your religion draw out of you?

Action: Pray to the Spirit each morning to bring you one of these fruits. Work throughout the day to achieve that virtue. Be mindful of the Holy Spirit and how he can help focus you on reaching that goal, especially when tested. At the end of the week, reflect on how you did.

21

The Spirit of Truth

Jesus only used two phrases to refer to the Holy Spirit. The first is that Greek word *parakletos*. It can be translated as "Comforter," "Helper," or "Advocate."

The second phrase is much clearer. No dual meanings. Jesus refers to the Holy Spirit as the "Spirit of truth." As in, "When the Helper comes . . . that is the Spirit of truth . . . He will testify about Me" (John 15:26). And in John 16:13–14, "When He, the Spirit of truth, comes, He will guide you into all the truth . . . He will glorify Me."

The only thing really left to consider is what is the truth? Jesus makes that clear in the quotes above. The Holy Spirit points back to Jesus himself. Jesus Christ is the only real truth.

Look back for a moment when Jesus first refers to the Holy Spirit. "If you love Me, you will keep My commandments. I will ask the Father, and He will give you another Helper" (John 14:15–16). Why does Jesus refer to the Spirit as "another" helper? Because he is the first helper. He is our first advocate.

Jesus arrived first. He gave up everything in heaven to come down to this lowly earth to humbly serve us, to submit to our mocking and torture, and be crucified, and suffer our deserved separation from his Father. He physically showed us how great is God's love. In sacrificing himself, Jesus justifies our reunion with the Holy Trinity in heaven and welcomes us into a blessed communion with them.

At The Last Supper, in the book of John, just before he was to die, the last thing Jesus does is pray for us. At the pinnacle of that prayer, he "advocates" for us to the Lord: "I do not ask on behalf of these alone [disciples], but for those who believe in Me through their word; that they may all be one; even as You, Father, are in Me and I in You, that they may also be in Us . . . Father, I desire that they also, whom You have given Me, be with Me where I am, so that they may see My glory which you have given Me, for You loved Me before the foundation of the world" (John 17: 20–24).

The Spirit is not our living sacrifice, but he points back to the one who was. The Spirit is here today to remind us of the real meaning of Jesus' sacrifice. The Holy Spirit is here to welcome us into holy communion with our God.

In a time of tragedy for me and my family, the Holy Spirit has been our great Comforter. We have felt his peace. But this is only the beginning. The Spirit is so much more.

When I look back at my dependence on the Spirit after the death of Nathan, I see that all the comfort he provided pointed toward Jesus Christ.

Nathan was prey to the evils of mental illness. He blindly tried to save himself from his demons. He could not control this world, and it failed him. Yet, all it took was a word to change his fate. In wearing that Led Zeppelin shirt, I believe he was crying out to God. Without Jesus' sacrifice, he would not be able to shine the white light of heaven. It all turns back to Jesus.

Nathan's stairway to heaven is not possible without Christ's sacrifice.

The constant reminders of Nathan's salvation in heaven. The reassurances that we receive from the Holy Spirit that Nathan is safe and at peace. None of it is possible without Jesus Christ.

The Spirit is with us now. And thankfully, so is Nathan. Every time the Spirit reminds me of this with a 42 moment, it is Jesus I have to thank for a message worth telling. For a son, still alive, and waiting for us all to reunite in heaven.

Psalm 23, as does the whole Bible, points directly back to Jesus. He is our Shepherd who has led the way before us. Through the valley of the shadow of death. He was killed by us—a sinless sacrifice—in order to pay a covenant with God that none of us are capable of on our own. He leads the way for us, he has been surrounded by our enemies before us, he has died, and he has traveled through that valley, leading the way to the light of heaven.

He is with us now, too, through the Holy Spirit's work.

It behooves us to remember that this is ultimately the purpose of the Holy Spirit. He is here to glorify God and redirect us to Jesus Christ. Just as Jesus came down to this earth to open our path to the Father, the Spirit is here now, alive in all of us, to open our eyes to Christ.

In another quote from The Last Supper, Jesus again tells us all what the Spirit means to us, "He will teach you all things, and bring to your remembrance all that I have said to you" (John 14:26).

Without the Spirit, there is no one drawing us to the Lord our Father and Jesus our Savior. We cannot begin to witness their love for us and practice it toward each other. There is no hope for us to be part of that selfless relationship of servitude with the Trinity God. We cannot experience his kingdom. We cannot see all he does for us here and prepares for us in heaven. And we will not experience all the treasures he gives us.

What a remarkable purpose the Spirit has. What a wonderful message to spread throughout the world.

But what an awesome task as well. We are stubborn people. We are constantly drawn away from the Lord, but the Spirit constantly calls us back. We are fortunate to have a God who does not give up on us. Who loves us enough, despite our many faults, to always welcome us back.

He sent us his perfect son to die and suffer the consequences of our sin that we might live. He has sent us the Holy Spirit, who yearns for our attention, begs for our community, and has this awesome gift in Jesus Christ to share with us.

May we ultimately find the means to listen, praise, and join him. The Spirit is here to glorify Christ that in his sacrifice we might be reunited with the whole Trinity through him. The Spirit is in us, so that we may understand the grace, love, and salvation

God provides. And so that we might radiate those facts toward others.

As Jesus said about the Spirit (John 15:26–27): "He will testify about Me, and you will testify also."

In the end, there is only one thing we can rely on, and that is God. To desire anything else is foolishness. C. S. Lewis puts it this way in *The Great Divorce*: "There is but one good; that is God. Everything else is good when it looks to him and bad when it turns from him."

James gives this instruction (Jas 4:7–8): "Resist the Devil and he will flee from you . . . . Cleanse your hands, you sinners; and purify your hearts, you double-minded." Do not allow yourself to be "double-minded."

Everything needs to point to God, or it will eventually disappoint you in its imperfections. Focus on the Holy Spirit, strive to get to know him as much as he wants to know you, make him a priority in your life, and all will be good. He will "restore your soul."

Remember, the Spirit is here with us now. He continues Jesus' teachings and works within us to guide our understanding of the Father and Christ. He works to foster our relationship with them.

Jesus said (John 14:23), "If anyone loves Me, he will keep My word; and My Father will love him, and We will come to him and make Our abode with him."

"We" refers to God the Father and the Son loving us from heaven, but they also make their home within us on earth in the form of the Holy Spirit. All three, working together to help us realize the truth and attain a perfect communion within their Trinity. As such, we become fully awash in their love. And with that comes all the comfort in the world.

Question: What do you worship in this life? What priority does God take in your life? Who is your God? Does God work to unite you with others or separate you?

Action: Renew your baptismal covenant with God. Read through the questions asked of your parents before committing you to God. Do you still believe all those statements? Does your life reflect those beliefs?

22

Infinite Love

About a year after Nathan died, Sarah and I met with our preacher at church. His profound advice resonates with me to this day. He said it is impossible to get through such tragedy without love.

He reminded us that the church is there to support us with love, but his words also reminded us to lean on each other, as well as our friends and community. Our communion with others and their caring and compassion toward our family is one of the few ways we were able to make it through this. People helped fill our hearts after Nathan died.

M. Scott Peck in his book *People of the Lie*, writes, "The only ultimate way to conquer evil is to let it be smothered within a willing, living human being. The healing of evil—scientifically or otherwise—can be accomplished only by the love of individuals."

My first response to our preacher was if only love can heal, then why not go to the ultimate source of love in the first place? Indeed, my greatest security and healing recently has come from God.

Augustine understood this. The early Christian saint was speaking in generalities, but his words are especially relevant in times of suffering: "If there is a God who created you, then the deepest chambers of your soul simply cannot be filled up by anything less."

For me, an intimate understanding of this truth is the greatest good that has come from Nathan's death. On this earth, I will never see him again, but God's love has overcome that tragic fact and offered me hope for the future.

The Bible speaks of love often. John writes in his first letter: "God is love. In this the love of God was made manifest among us, that God sent his only Son into the world" (1 John 4:8–9). Not only is God actually love, but Jesus was the perfect manifestation of that love on earth.

Before Nathan died, I experimented with the Gospels. I read them, but substituted the word "love" for Jesus. It helped me understand some of what Jesus means to us.

Take the Book of John for example. "In the beginning was Love, and Love was with God, and Love was God. Love was in the beginning with God. All things came into being through Love . . . Love shines in the darkness, and the darkness did not comprehend it" (John 1:1–5).

Indeed, even before time, the Trinity existed as a perfect example of love. Love is perhaps the best way to describe what abides between the Father, Son, and Holy Spirit in their service to each other.

That love permeates the example of Jesus' life. He lived in love for God and others. This is certainly how he was trying to teach us to live. "Love is the bread of life" (John 6:35). "Love is the light of the world" (John 8:12). "Love is the way, and the truth, and the life" (John 14:6). Loving is certainly a critically good start.

In many ways, we are now manifestations of God's love as well. As God's temple, through the Holy Spirit, we need to reflect that love.

Jesus' greatest commandment for us was to love. "Love the Lord your God." And secondly, "Love your neighbor."

Today, I get joy from helping my patients through their struggles. I soak in my experiences with Sarah and remaining son and daughter incredibly, and I have no problem expressing the love I have for them.

I can more easily appreciate that godly love in others too. I am joyful in my interactions with their faithfulness, kindness, concerns, and sympathy. It is all very good to me.

God created us to love, and it is the best image of God we can display. As we tap into the presence of the Holy Spirit and recognize his purpose to glorify Jesus through us, it is love that is the primary manifestation of that presence.

Specifically, love has served three purposes for me in my time of healing. First, it increases my suffering. How much I hurt these days is a direct reflection of how much I loved Nathan. I still think of Nathan daily and that often leads to frustration, guilt, and terrible sadness. I still miss him dearly and ache to see him again. That element of grief never goes away.

Second, my love for him is a source of peace. I know I loved Nathan with all my heart when he was here. It was not enough, but I tried. This eases a lot of my guilt. Sometimes all you can do is to love those around you as best as you are able.

Finally, love fills the emptiness that has been left by Nathan's absence. Nathan is safe and secure now, surrounded by more love than I can possibly imagine. What little of God's love I feel connected to and am able to access is far more than my suffering. This brings me peace, joy, and goodness. Like you, I have been blessed by God's presence.

Hopefully, my experiences, and this book will help you focus your love for those around you and be a more complete and positive influence for them. I hope it helps you be more deliberate, persistent, and beneficial in your actions. And I hope you are able to tap into that infinite love that God reserves for just you. May you find communion with God's Spirit in you.

I cannot imagine going through my suffering without the Spirit at my side. He has been invaluable as my Comforter. He is my source of God's love.

But we need to remember that the Spirit is also our source of God's Truth. I must confess, my experiment to replace Jesus with "Love" in the Gospels only worked about half of the time. That is because Jesus is much more to us than just the perfect personification of God's love. He is also our Savior. He came down to earth to die for our sins and open the gates of heaven to all of us. None of us are worthy without him.

Jesus manifests God's love in his suffering as well as his goodness. "For God so loved the world, that He gave His only Son, that whoever believes in Him shall not perish, but have eternal life" (John 3:16).

"We know love by this, that He laid down His life for us" (1 John 3:16). And, "Greater love has no one than this, that they lay down his life for his friends" (John 15:13).

Jesus leads us in the ways of suffering. He understands, sympathizes, and comforts us. We, however, cannot model, repay, or even completely understand this level of love. All we can do is lean on him and be thankful. And do our best to glorify this incredible sacrifice.

John's gospel cannot be completely understood from just the perspective of love. Jesus himself is necessary. "I am the resurrection and the life; he who believes in Me will live even if he dies" (John 11:25). Love might be the beginning. But Jesus is the beginning and the end. The Alpha and the Omega.

Remember, without the Spirit, there is no understanding of God, no relationship with him, and ultimately no life within our souls. Without the Spirit, there is no one drawing us to the Lord our Father and Jesus our Savior. The Spirit guides us to their love for us and helps us practice it toward each other. He enables us to be part of the selfless, loving relationship of servitude with the Trinity God. And freely gives us all the treasures of heaven.

May God's Spirit bless you with this truth.

Question: Think of a person who you have a hard time getting along with or who rubs you the wrong way. Perhaps it is a family member, or a work colleague, or someone with different political views, or who practices another religion. Can you see God in any part of that person? Can you see the heavenly nature that God created in them? Perhaps it is not in their kindness or good will, but in their suffering that they resemble Jesus? Perhaps it is in their pain?

Action: Read one of the Gospels. How would Jesus respond to that person you are thinking of? How does he respond to you? How do you reflect what he is teaching you?

Epilogue 3

"Now faith, hope, love, abide these three; but the greatest of these is love" (1 Cor 13:13).

God blesses you with faith in this world, hope for the future, and love for each other.

Embrace them all.

Resources

American Suicide Prevention Lifeline (24/7): 800-273-8255

American Foundation for Suicide Prevention: www.afsp.org

Suicide Awareness/Voices of Education: www.save.org

Suicide Prevention Resource Center: www.sprc.org